Deep the Water, Shallow the Shore

Deep the Water, Shallow the Shore

Three Essays on Shantying in the West Indies

Roger D. Abrahams

Music Transcribed by Linda Sobin

MYSTIC SEAPORT MUSEUM, INC.
Mystic, Connecticut
2002

Mystic Seaport
75 Greenmanville Ave., P. O. Box 6000
Mystic, CT 06355-0990

Cataloging-in-Publication Data

Abrahams, Roger D.
        Deep the water, shallow the shore.
        1. Folk-songs–West Indies, British–History and
criticism. 2. Sea songs.
I. Title.
ML3565.A27   2002   784.6'8'6238
ISBN 0-913372-98-6

To my parents, Nevisian-Americans

CONTENTS

LIST OF SONGS WITH MUSIC

FOREWORD

"Nowhere is the complexity of the study of folksongs so well illustrated as in shantying"* says Roger Abrahams in his first chapter of this volume. That "complexity," and particularly the African influence upon it, has fascinated us on the music staff at Mystic Seaport for years. Abrahams goes on to hint at the possibility that contact between European sailors and Afro-American communities may have spawned much of the chantey tradition we have come to know.

The reason behind the complexity that Abrahams so rightly proclaims is that, for all the ages of civilization between the papyrus raft and the airplane, ships carrying cargo were the fluid transport of culture as well as goods. Why? Because, from the earliest days, not only were these vessels touching new ground and entirely new populations, but they were also appropriating members of these populations as they required sailors to replace those who had died or deserted. Throughout the history of deep-water sail, there have been polyglot crews. And those crews, shar-

---

*Note: There are several accepted spellings for the central term in this study. "Shanty" as used by Dr. Abrahams is most common among the majority of collectors, with a plural of shanties, but Cecil Sharp in 1914 used "chantey(s)," as did Frederick Pease Harlow in his *Chanteying Aboard American Ships* (1962), but with a plural of chanties. Harlow points out the French root of *chanter* (to sing) for his preference, but Abrahams choice of shanty is particularly appropriate for the islands where he collected these songs, as they might occasionally be employed when moving an abode of the same name.

ing the cramped quarters of the fo'c'sle as well as the dangers and distresses of life at sea, must have shared some elements of their various backgrounds, the most accessible of which would have been music. Unfortunately, much of that fertile exchange has been lost, and now we must turn to our best resources for evidence. In our own search, we at Mystic Seaport have brought to our annual Sea Music Festival the Menhaden Chanteymen from North Carolina and the Buckingham Lining Bar Gang from Virginia to demonstrate recent African-American work-song traditions from the fisheries and railroad labor. We have also benefited from the research of former Mystic Seaport chanteyman Bob Walser at the Library of Congress, and more recently in England. And we have listened with delight to recent rereleases on CD of material from the Alan Lomax collection and others of music from African-American traditions and the Caribbean.

But best of all, we have turned back to our cherished out-of-print copies of this Roger Abrahams 1974 volume. Within these pages, captured while they were still being actively employed in the fishing and whaling trades, are songs that reveal fascinating links between deep-water chanteying and these island occupations, and epitomize a process of adaptation that is as old as human experience on the sea. For me, this collection is one of our finest touchstones to the powerful tradition of the work song at sea.

GEOFF KAUFMAN

PREFACE 2002

The songs included in these essays record the coming together of representatives of many different peoples on board ships engaged in international trade. A volatile mixture of representatives of different cultures, they often found themselves coordinated in their work through the performance of Africans and African Americans who came from the great call-and-response shouting traditions. Working people, not always shipping out by their own choice, careered on the waters, moving goods from port to port, loading and unloading them in the same responsory singing style as they used to carry out the tasks on board. And they used the same songs with altered stanzas in a number of the other working situations discussed in the first essay. Even the field slaves of the American South drew upon some of these songs in their gang-work in the fields. In a book reporting the widespread ceremony of the corn-shucking in the American South, *Singing the Master*, I report many of the same songs sung in the same shouted form.

These songs, then, were carried out in African style, but used in a number of situations in which European and American entrepreneurs were the primary beneficiaries. Most obviously, the owners and masters of the ships prospered in part by drawing on the vocal power of the great shouters to bring their efforts toward efficient handling of ship and cargo into order vibrantly. These bow-legged bastards themselves had developed a body of song out of the necessity of having been thrown together.

Making a virtue of the necessity of coordinating work or dying in the process, they used these songs to get through certain on-board tasks that were so chancy that to miss a beat too often meant disfiguring accidents or worse. Adopting the classic sub-Saharan ways of singing to coordinate their energies, whether they were from the Black Atlantic world or not, whalers and other sailors hauled and pushed, furled and pulled, all the while reminding each other what they were doing together. As with many such thrown-together groups, there were those geniuses of invention among them who shouted the words that urged each other on. Drawing on the song style characteristic of work performances throughout Africa and the Greater Caribbean, with the responsive interlocking and overlapping of voices and gestures, the songs commented directly on the problems of trying to wrest a living from the sea.

As a folksinger in the 1950s, for me the sea shanty represented a body of song that compelled us to sing together, but which had to be learned from the few old folk survivors of the "great days of whaling and sailing." The songs themselves had been caught on the fly, as the singers and the tradition itself were dying. In fact, they were artifacts of that world which were sufficiently compelling that they made their way into the elementary school repertoire, sung by those upward striving American kids a world away from that in which a "Blow the Man Down" could only be imagined from the experience of flying a kite, and Shenandoah and his daughter were of the same tribe as Pocahontas, Squanto, and Tonto. If we came to understand the toil that lay behind the songs, it was not through the experiences themselves, but from reading about them in *Moby-Dick* or *Two Years Before the Mast*.

This book itself emerged through serendipity. The great record producer and field collector, Kenneth S. Goldstein, and I were longtime friends. Kenny and I went to graduate school together, where we had the opportunity to discuss the English language folk-song repertoire all of the time. No traditions were more central to our shared concerns that those attached to work.

Kenny, even after entering graduate school, continued to edit the long-playing recordings for which he became so famed. Among other projects, he edited and issued a recording of a group of revival folksingers—Paul Clayton, Dave Van Ronk, Bob Yellin, Bob Brill, and myself—singing shanties that Paul had garnered from the BBC folk-song archive and taught to the rest of us (which is still available, under the title *Paul Clayton and the Fo'c'stle Singers*, from Smithsonian-Folkways).

When I went to the West Indies in the early 1960s to carry out fieldwork, I discovered that many of the questions folk-song revival singers and scholars had asked could now be answered by talking with working sailors themselves, such as the singers I encountered in the various fishing communities in which I worked on Nevis, Tobago, and St. Vincent. When I first discovered these traditions were still being used, naturally I shared my excitement with Kenny, writing him and sending the essays that were beginning to emerge from these forays. Our research had long suggested that West Indians were among the most important shantymen (a point that shantyman and performer Stan Hugill made in many of his public presentations). I sent Kenny early drafts of the three articles. He was the editor of the American Folklore Society Memoir Series at the time, and he wrote back saying that he thought they made the kind of nice, tidy little book that he would like to issue for the Society. It was a few years before the book was actually issued, published by the University of Texas Press, which was then in a contractual relationship with the AFS. The transcriptions of the songs, by Linda Sobin, were accomplished when I returned to my teaching duties at the University of Texas.

When I went to teach with Kenny at the University of Pennsylvania in 1985, the administrator of the Folklore and Folklife Department, Theresa Pyott, asked me if I knew that some of the songs from the book were being sung by a revival shanty group at various festivals of the sea. She put me in touch with one of these groups, and it seemed like a happy connection was made. I sent them a copy of the tapes of the St. Vincent whalers, indicating that I was pleased to have the songs well cared for. Subsequently, I made copies for a number of other shanty-fiends.

Now, nearly forty years later, I find myself reviewing those days, and reliving some of the experiences. In 2001, I was contacted by Ken Bilby, the renowned Afro-Americanist, who asked me to edit a CD of the songs that Alan Lomax and I had collected in 1962, many of which are included in the second essay here. It will be issued sometime in 2002 by Rounder Records.

It is humbling to return to one's earlier voice and to the experience of recording the geniuses of invention who were then still working the sea-lanes of the Caribbean. It is nothing to become a song-catcher in this area of the world, for vernacular invention lies at the core of West Indian life.

And now the folks at Mystic Seaport have made it possible for these essays to be reprinted as part of their efforts as the Museum of America and the Sea. More than that, some of the singers I worked with in 1966 were discovered still alive and singing. So we will have a reunion of sorts in June 2002, when they will perform as part of the annual Sea Music Festival at Mystic Seaport. I thank the Mystic Seaport crew, especially Geoff Kaufman, for bringing off this event.

PREFACE TO THE 1974 EDITION

There are certain musical types that seem to arise only in areas in which Afro-Americans and Euro-Americans perform together or at least witness each other's performance forms–jazz, jody calls, cheerleading, to use some American examples. The sea shanty is one of these. In chanter-response performance type, with a high degree of voice overlap and interlock, these work songs are more in African singing style than European (with the possible exception of Celtic singing in groups). Yet they arose and thrived at a time when Afro- and Euro-Americans and Europeans worked together under sail, and it seems clear that it was this combination of ethnic groups pursuing a common purpose that provided the situation under which these songs thrived.

Herein are three essays concerned with the West Indian contribution to this exchange, a contribution much attested to by the sailors themselves but not much noted in the recent literature on the subject. Shanties are still being sung in many parts of the Anglophonic Caribbean, and those communities in which they are still being employed provide us with the bulk of the materials included here.

These essays do not attempt to solve the problem of origins. They do attempt to permit a fuller understanding of the problem by showing, first, how the song type was associated in the minds of English-speaking travelers with Afro-Americans, specifically with West Indians; second, how the pattern of coordinated chanter-response singing while working persists in the area; and, third, how that contemporary song tradition has been affected by the international sailing trade.

I am indebted to many who have helped along the way. The geographer Dr. John A. Adams was the first to lead me to the whalers at Barouallie, and he supplied me with a great deal of insight and information. Even more helpful in regard to this community was John Sullivan, a Peace Corps worker in the town, who has studied the blackfish whaling and whalers in an attempt to make that practice more economically feasible. Were he not so reticent, the third chapter would appear as co-authored by him. I am indebted to Mr. Clifford Arendell of Barouallie for telling me about the blackfishing from his own infinite personal and local knowledge.

I have had long and excellent conversations with Alan Lomax about shanties and shantying, and I am more deeply in his debt on such social and stylistic matters than can be expressed here. His cantometric analyses have provided many important insights. He made some excellent recordings of the Newcastle, Nevis, fishermen, which he has kindly shared with me, though the songs reported here from these fishermen came from my own forays.

Thomas A. Green has done valuable transcribing for me. As indicated on the title page, Linda Sobin transcribed the songs with great care and pleasant enthusiasm. Frances Terry and Marilyn Sandlin typed the many versions of the manuscript. To all these, my thanks.

Deep the Water, Shallow the Shore

1. Shantying in the West Indies

Many have lamented the death of sea shantying, but the practice is far from dead. Shantying is throughout the Caribbean, especially in areas in which English Creole is spoken, the sung dimension of virtually any group endeavor calling for coordination of strength. The songs may be improvised for the occasion, or, more commonly, they may come from the international store of shanties including those associated with the sea trades in the days of the large sailing vessels. There are shanties, such as "Caesar Boy, Caesar," "Bulldog, Don't Bite Me," and "Bell-a Ring," which seem never to have been sung beyond the Caribbean rim. Others which are reported to have originated here, such as "Hanging Johnny" and "Fire Down Below," became a part of the repertoire of all sailing men; all of these are still being sung, no longer in relation to hauling anchor or work at the capstan but as encouragement for moving a house or pushing a fishing boat back in the ocean after the hurricane season. Thus, long after the big sailing ships have put into Ilo, Chile, one can hear West Indians—men, women, or children—singing "Johnny Come Down to Hilo" while hauling a heavy cauldron from one yard to another; as a rowing song in the fishing operation; or, as on St. Vincent, to accompany the game of "pong finger" in which large stones or coconut husks are passed, rhythmically, around the ring of seated people, each person trying to "pong" (pound) the hand of the next.

"Johnny Come Down with a Hilo"

The poor old man he sick in bed.
He want somebody to 'noint his head.
Oh, Johnny come down with a hilo,
A poor old man.

Similarly, one can hear "Yankee John, Stormaline" or "Boney Was a Warrior" sung by workers coordinating a hoeing operation or a version of "Do My Johnny Booker" used for lifting a house onto a truck, as on Nevis:

From Halifax to Dover
Is ninety miles and over,
Do my jolly boy',

"Do My Jolly Boy'"

♩=120

SHANTYMAN

From Ha - li - fax to Do — ver is nine-ty miles and o — ver,

SINGERS

Do my jol-ly boy', Bul - lie', are we de'?

Ayy (Shout)   Oh yo.

Long and strong, me hear-ty boys, Bul-lies, long and strong,

Oh yo.

Repeat 3 times
then D.C. al fine

Shub 'e shub an' le' we go,

Oh yo.   Oh yo.   Fine

* ALTERNATIVE

(Together) Ayy.

Bullie', are we de'?
(Together) Oh yo.
Long and strong, me hearty boys,
(Together) Oh yo.

Bullies, long and strong,
Oh yo.
Shub 'e shub, an' le' we go,
Oh yo.

Bullie', le' we go,
Oh yo.
Shub along an' le' we go,
Oh yo.

Bullie', come we go,
Oh yo.
Long an' strong me hearty boys,
Oh yo.

From Halifax to Dover
Is ninety miles and over,
Do my jolly boy',
(Together) Ayy.

Bullie', le' we go,
Oh yo.
Long an' strong me hearty boys,
Oh yo.

Bullie' shanty strong,
Oh yo.
Shub dis house an' le' we go,
Oh yo.
(Spoken) Two blocks.   *(signals the end of the job)*

But these songs are not the only ones used for such purposes in the British Caribbean. New songs are still being created, which comment on recent local events and personages; or songs that tell of ancient doings but that have never achieved international provenience can be heard. Nowhere is the complexity of the study of the distribution of folksongs so well illustrated as in shantying, for here one can observe the purely local and the international song existing side by side; in some cases the international composition began in this area and in other cases it came from far away. Furthermore, there is a continuing and haunting question of whether the practice of shantying was ever common to the deep-sea trades before extended contacts of European sailors with Afro-American communities.

Most collectors and commentators on shanties say something about the influence of black traditions, though there is no agreement on the extent or the origins of this influence. W. F. Arnold, commenting on the music of the shanties from the repertoire of F. T. Bullen, states boldly that "the majority of the chanties are negroid in origin" and goes on to describe the evidence as he sees it.[1] Cecil Sharp calls this a "vexed question" but admits nonetheless that "the negro has undoubtedly left his impression upon a certain number of chantey-tunes." This influence, he notes, is only natural "when we remember that sailing ships, engaged in the Anglo-American trade, commonly carried 'chequered' crews, *i.e.* one watch of coloured men and one of white."[2] Other reporters amplify one or another facet of the "vexing" question. For instance, Joanna Colcord says that a number of songs in the Anglo-American repertoire came from the Negro stevedores in American gulf ports, "songs developed as an aid to stowing cotton, the bales being rammed tightly into the ship's hold by means of heavy wooden wedges. As the shanties proved useful, either for hauling or for the windlass, they were picked up by the ships' crews and became part of the shantyman's repertoire." But she is quick to note, rightly, of this tradition that "there were numberless others of

[1] F. T. Bullen and W. F. Arnold, *Songs of Sea Labour*, p. xiii.
[2] Cecil Sharp, *English Folk-Chanteys*, p. xv.

the same kind, extemporized by Negro singers, which did not attain any wide popularity."[3]

Charles Nordhoff describes how this contact of traditions was established in his account of having shipped to Mobile Bay in the late 1840's, where he watched, fascinated, the loading of the cotton.

> . . . so great is the force applied that not unfrequently the ship's decks are raised off the stancheons which support them, and the seams are torn violently asunder. . . . The gang . . . takes hold of the handles of the screws, the foreman begins the song, and at the end of every two lines the worm of the screw is forced to make one revolution. . . . Singing, or *chanting* as it is called, is an invariable accompaniment to working in cotton, and many of the screw-gangs have an endless collection of songs . . . answering well the purposes of making all pull together, and enlivening the heavy toil. The foreman is the *chantyman*, who sings the song, the gang only joining in the chorus, which comes in at the end of every line, and at the end of which again comes the pull of the screw handles.
>
> The chants . . . have more of rhyme than reason in them. The tunes are generally plaintive . . . as are most of the capstan tunes of sailors, but resounding over the still waters . . . they had a fine effect.[4]

In similar fashion, William Doerflinger emphasizes the influence of Afro-Americans on the shanty repertoire. "No one can fail to notice the many touches of Negro song even in shanties traditional among white sailor-men. Since before the days of the cotton trade, American Negroes had enjoyed a special reputation as talented singers. . . . There were no finer shantymen, as a class, than the Negroes, whose racial gifts of song, dance, and humor also made them particularly popular as dogwatch entertainers."[5]

It is difficult to discern why these commentators should have so

---

[3] Joanna Colcord, *Songs of American Sailormen*, p. 59.

[4] Charles Nordhoff, *Nine Years a Sailor* (noted in William Doerflinger, *Shantymen and Shantyboys*, p. 98).

[5] Doerflinger, p. 97.

emphasized the influence of the Negro from the United States on the practice and the repertoire when there was so great a commerce with the West Indian communities, especially among the whalers. Of the American and British collectors only the songs from Jamaican sailors given by James Hatfield in 1946 and the more recent works by Stan Hugill and Frederick Pease Harlow take note of West Indian shantying traditions. Hugill states boldly that, "although the West Indian is rarely referred to by writers on shantying, I feel that he was responsible for producing far more seamen's work-songs than any Negro of the Southern States of America. West Indian Negroes have shipped as seamen and cooks in our merchant ships and naval vessels from the earliest times and were ever to the fore as shanty men."[6] He includes a number of songs from West Indian provenience, as does Harlow. The latter not only has a number of songs from a 'Badian singer but also includes a characteristic description of a visit to Barbados in 1878.

> The negro stevedores at the fall where the cargo was hoisted by hand, sang [*Hanging Johnny*] day after day, using words for all relations, including hanging the baby as well as the bull pup, the pigs and the goats. The harmony of their voices outshone any college quartet ever heard. It was a stand-off between *Hanging Johnny* and *I Love the Blue Mountains of Tennessee* as to which they liked best.
>
> It was in the month of June and those negroes worked in the hot sun, singing away as they worked, until the leading chantyman was out of breath, only to be relieved by another nearly his equal. Such singing I never expect to hear again under similar conditions.
>
> . . . I recall a deck scene under a tropical sun at Bridgetown Barbados, where worked four negroes at the fall, their faces shone from perspiration that stood out like silvery beads against their black skin.
>
> The leading chantyman wore a red bandana handkerchief tied loosely around his neck and flowing over his shoulders partly covered with a dungaree jumper which was unbuttoned at the throat, expos-

[6] Stan Hugill, *Shanties from the Seven Seas*, p. 8.

ing his black skin devoid of underclothing and polished ebony. The whites of his eyes shone brightly as he pulled at the fall and the whipcords in his neck stood out like a pair of swifters showing the strain he was under as he sang hour after hour. He improvised words as only a negro poet could, at times so comical as to cause his companions to laugh heartily when forced to use too many words in the metre to make up the rhyme. They were a happy lot and good stevedores so long as they chantyed. But without the chanty they were too lazy to get out of their own way.[7]

If the shanty collectors neglected to mention the importance of the West Indian tradition, travelers to that area were struck by these improvised work songs. And they betrayed, as did Harlow, their real interest in such songs, for they often were concerned with whether these Afro-Americans were as they had been described—childish and lazy, animalistic and happy. Specifically, there was a good deal of discussion by these travelers as to whether these people were capable of being "civilized"; these considerations caused the commentators to point out certain performance traits, revolving around the Negro stereotype, that otherwise might have gone unnoticed. Interesting in this regard is the commentary by "A Naval Officer" who visited the West Indies early in the 1830's.

> Some have remarked on the little aptitude or taste evinced in music, inferring a deficiency of the faculty: but the remark will apply to all barbarous people; the talent is probably one of civilisation, and with the negro only requires the cultivation of the innate germ to make it fructify. Some of their airs are exceedingly plaintive, and the

[7] Frederick Pease Harlow, *Chanteying Aboard American Ships*, pp. 241–242. Richard Runciman Terry, arguing in *The Shanty Book*, part I, vi, that the word "shanty" comes from West Indian housemoving ceremonies, tacitly admits a West Indian influence. C. Fox Smith, in *A Book of Shanties*, pp. 11–14, argues against the housemoving theory; he suggests that there were fiddlers on board, who were responsible for these songs, one of whom was "emphatically a gentleman of colour," a West Indian. Laura A. Smith, in *Music of the Waters*, surveys the sea songs of the world but has nothing on the West Indies whatsoever.

manner of singing in chorus evinces no small degree of natural taste: rowing in boats or other kind of labour, when a simultaneous effort is required, they have generally a song formed of extempore verses, the improvisatore being the stroke oar, the driver, or one supereminent among the rest for the talent. He in a minor key gives out a line or two in allusion to any passing event, all the rest taking up the burthen of the song, as a chorus, in a tenor, and this produces a very pleasing effect. For instance, at the Virgin Islands, the boatman's song is as follows:—

> Jenny go to market for buy me varrow prantin,
> Heigh me know, bombye me takey.
> CHORUS—Heigh me know &c.
> Heigh me know &c.

> Me nebur know, before Jenny bin a bad gal,
> Heigh me know, bombye me takey.
> CHORUS—Heigh me know, &c.
> Heigh me know, &c.

At Antigua:—

> Massa lock de door, and take away de key,
> Hurra, my jolly boys, grog time a day.
> CHORUS—Grog time a day, my boys, grog time a day,
> Hurra, my jolly boys, grog time a day, &c.[8]

A number of early visitors to the region commented at some length on this manner of singing as an accompaniment to all kinds of tasks that called for coordination and the mark of good cheer that the songs gave. The earliest report of this kind of singing comes from William Beckford's *Descriptive Account of the Island of Jamaica*, which was published in London in 1790. He too was taken with the "plaintive" sound of these work songs, though, strangely enough, his report refers only to the singing of women:

[8] *Service Afloat.*

When the mill is at work at night, there is something affecting in
the songs of the women who feed it; and it appears somewhat singular, that all their tunes, if tunes they can be called, are of a plaintive
cast. Sometimes you may hear one soft, complaining voice; and now
a second and a third chime in; and presently, as if inspired by the
solemn impressions of night, and by the gloomy objects that are supposed to dwell around, a full chorus is heard to swell upon the ear, and
then to die away again to the first original tone.

The style of singing among the negroes, is uniform: and this is
confined to the women; for the men very seldom, excepting upon
extraordinary occasions, are ever heard to join in chorus. One person
begins first, and continues to sing alone; but at particular periods the
others join: there is not, indeed, much variety in their songs; but
their intonation is not less perfect than their time.[9]

There are a number of such descriptions in later works, most often
associated with harvest scenes, for that was the time of greatest
activity on the plantations in the West Indies. One writer, Trelawny
Wentworth, was carried away with the bucolic implications of such
a scene, and in his rush of emotion he provides us not only with a full
description of the activities but also with one of the songs performed
by the slaves.

It would be difficult to convey an adequate idea of the very lively
and imposing character of a West Indian harvest, combined with all
the sublimity and loveliness of tropical scenery, and a tropical atmos-
phere: even slavery appears divested of its obnoxious and compli-
cated character amidst the festivity and mirth which prevail; and
such is the nourishing property of the sugar-cane, that the negroes,
who consume great quantities of it, never appear so healthy and ani-
mated as at this particular season; it has a wonderful and immediate
effect upon their whole system, frequently restoring the weak and
sickly to the enjoyment of health and spirits.

The dwelling of the proprietor, or his attorney, is usually situated

[9] William Beckford, *A Descriptive Account of the Island of Jamaica*, II, 120–
121.

on an elevation to windward, in the vicinity of the works, to afford a commanding view over the estate, and to facilitate communication with the stores and hospital, as well as more immediate control over the labour carried on at the mill and boiling-house. From this point, during the season of which we are speaking, is witnessed a scene of animation and cheerfulness, corresponding in character with that which is passing in the field; and we have often been constrained to listen to the light-hearted hilarity of the negroes, and to watch, with infinite satisfaction, the gambols of the rising generation, pelting each other with the macerated cane, which they are employed to strew in the sun to dry for fuel, after it has passed through the mill. The carts passing and repassing in conveying the bundles of canes from the field, the negroes transporting the canes to the mill, the mill vanes rustling in their revolution, and the confused clamour of voices in dialogue and song, present a singular contrast to that calm repose which nature seems to claim for herself in these clear and ardent climes, manifesting only at intervals her indignant wrath in hurricanes and earthquakes, as if impatient of the presence of man. Here is a song, or rather a *chorus*, which the negroes sing on such occasions, being a fair sample of their poetry and music; kept up, perhaps, by a few of them working together, whilst the others at the same time sing some popular English tune, recently imported, forming together, something like that delectable compound of harmony and discord, a "Dutch Medley."

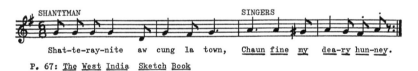

SHANTYMAN   SINGERS

Shat-te-ray-nite aw cung la town,   Chaun fine my dea-ry hun-ney.

P. 67: *The West India Sketch Book*

> Shat-te-ray-nite aw cung la town,
>   Chaun fine my dea-ry hun-ney.
> Aw run roun da lemon tree,
>   Chaun fine my deary hunney.
> Aw look behine da guaba bush,
>   Chaun fine my deary hunney.

Aw wash my pot, aw wash um clean,
Chaun fine my deary hunney.
Aw put in pease, aw put in poke,
Chaun fine my deary hunney.
Aw boil my pot, aw boil um sweet,
Chaun fine my deary hunney.
Aw sweep my house, aw sweep um clean,
Chaun fine my deary hunney.
Aw clean my nife, aw clean um shine,
Chaun fine my deary hunney.
Aw mek my bed, aw mek um soff,
Chaun fine my deary hunney.
Aw mak um up, aw shek um up,
Chaun fine my deary hunney.[10]

The reference in the refrain to "chaun fine" is probably what the author heard for "shant' fine," a phrase still heard from members of the chorus as encouragement to the singing leader.

Throughout the West Indies today, this type of song is primarily associated with two activities, fishing and whaling (where the songs are sung while rowing or while taking the boats in and out of the water) and housemoving. According to a number of authorities, it was housemoving that gave the songs their names, since the houses were named "shanties" (according to these authorities) and the leader would perch on top of the structure giving heart to his fellow workers.[11] Whether true or not, the travel literature once again provides us with an affecting description of this work as done on Antigua in the 1830's and 40's.

It most frequently happens, that the possessors of these small tenements have no land of their own, but pay a small ground-rent for the space occupied by their habitations. When they are wishful of

---

[10] Trelawny Wentworth, *The West India Sketch Book*, I, 65–66.
[11] See the résumé of this argument given by Stan Hugill, p. 22.

removing to another part of town, like the snail, they carry their houses with them, which, from the manner of construction, is no difficult matter. . . .

When a removal is agreed upon, their first care is to hire a few porters, and an accompaniment of trucks. These "four-wheelee" carriages are firmly fastened together, and placed under the house, the slight foundation pulled away, and strong ropes being attached to the first truck, the porters (with the assistance of other men, women, and children) commence pulling with all their might, and the house moves off to the song and chorus adapted to the occasion. To preserve its equilibrium, two men march on each side of the house with long poles, which they place against the side; one of these commences a song, (which is of their own composition) and the whole tribe join in the chorus of "Pull away, my hearties," or similar phrases. . . .

In former times, when the negroes had only the Sunday allowed them to perform any of their own work, that day was used to execute these removals; but the noise it occasioned during the period of divine service was such that the legislature found it necessary to prohibit this practice at the same time they abolished the Sunday markets.

It is particularly disagreeable to be in the vicinity of these houses when their owners take it into their heads to remove them. The negroes are always noisy; but when such deeds are in contemplation, they are more so than ever; the songs they sing, the quarrels they have, and the language they use would tire the patience of the most stoical. Sometimes a crash is heard and the whole edifice comes to the ground; this leads to a "wordy war,"—the goddess Discord again waves aloft her arm,—the whole neighborhood is in commotion.[12]

The earliest reporting of a song identified with the shantying tradition is given us by the expert Stan Hugill in a reference to "a voyage to Jamaica on the *Edward* merchantman, in the year 1811." But,

---

[12] [Mrs. Lanaghan], *Antigua and the Antiguans, A Full Account of the Colony and Its Inhabitants from the Time of the Caribs to the Present Day, Interspersed with Anecdotes and Legends*, II, 133–135.

once again, the song that is given is not identified with the sea trade but with shore work:

> Our seamen having left the ship, the harbour work was performed by a gang of Negroes. These men will work the whole day at the capstan under a scorching sun with almost no intermission. They beguiled the time by one of them singing one line of an English song, or a prose sentence at the end of which all the rest join in a short chorus. The sentences which prevail with the gang we had aboard were as follows:

> > Two sisters courted one,
> > *Ch.* Oh, huro, my boys,
> > And they live in the mountains,
> > *Ch.* Oh, huro boys O.

> And the second:

> > Grog time of day, boys,
> > Grog time of day,
> > *Ch.* Huro, my jolly boys,
> > Grog time of day.[13]

The literature of West Indian travelers provides no answers to the problems confronted by Hugill: when did shantying first begin on board the ships at sea, and where did the shanties come from? Two quotations from the 1830's, however, indicate that certain songs firmly associated with the sea trades were in active circulation among West Indian workers, but as rowing songs. The earliest of these, from Captain J. E. Alexander's *Transatlantic Sketches*, reports a trip up the Roraima River in British Guiana in 1831.

> I again proceeded into the bush, to visit an Indian settlement and the Tappacoona Lake, eight miles in length, formed by a dam between two sand hills, and intended to irrigate the Morocco estate in the event of a scarcity of rain. The negroes merrily plied the paddles, and

[13] Hugill, p. 8. The second song is the same as that reported in *Service Afloat*.

we brushed past the overhanging trees to their favorite song of "Velly well, yankee, velly well oh!"

> De bottley oh! de bottley oh!
> De neger like de bottley oh!
> Right early in de morning, de neger like de
> bottley oh!
> A bottle o' rum, loaf a bread,
> Make de neger dandy oh!
> Right early in de morning, de neger like de
> bottley oh![14]

The second account is provided by the indefatigable Trelawny Wentworth who not only describes the activities of the rowers at greater length but also gives us the music to the song.

For some distance they had pulled at an easy rate and in silence, as if made unconscious of the work they were engaged in, but the absorbing interest of the passing scenes, but at length they were roused to activity by the word of preparation for a song having been passed among them, and the negro pulling the oar nearest to us, began a singular prelude which sounded between a grunt and a groan, like a pavior's accompaniment to his labour, or the exordium of a quaker, when "the spirit" begins to move. He became more energetic with each succeeding stroke of the oar, which produced a corresponding ardour, and the greater precision in pulling among the other rowers, and when this was effected, another negro, whose countenance bore the stamp of much covert humour and sagacity, and who appeared to be a sort of *improvisatore* among them, commenced a lively strain

---

[14] Captain J. E. Alexander, *Transatlantic Sketches*, I, 130–131. The songs referred to are not one but, in all probability, two, the first a mishearing of "Bear Away Yankee, Bear Away, Oh" and the second "So Early in the Morning" or "The Sailor Likes His Bottle-O." See Hugill, pp. 56–57. (This reporting is much earlier than any he gives there.) Thomas Staunton St. Clair (*A Residence in the West Indies and America*, II, 152) gives another account of this singing and rowing, but says that they "sing in chorus the most absurd verses composed by themselves to keep up their spirits."

which accorded exactly in time with the motion of pulling, each line of the song accompanying the impetus given to the boat, and the whole crew joining in chorus in the intervals between every stroke of the oars. The subject matter of the song was as discursive and lengthy as Chevy Chase; and it showed an aptitude at invention on the part of the leader, as well as a tolerable acquaintance with the weak side of human nature, on the score of flattery: a small portion of it will suffice. The words in italics form the chorus.

"Fine Time o' Day"

Hur-ra my jol-ly boys, *Fine time o' day.* We pull for San Tha-mas, boys,

Fine time o' day.

P. 240: *The West India Sketch Book*

Hur-ra my jol-ly boys,
    Fine time o' day.
We pull for San Thamas, boys,
    Fine time o' day.
San Thamas hab de fine girl,
    Fine time o' day.
Nancy Gibbs and Betsy Braid,
    Fine time o' day.
Massa cum fro London town,
    Fine time o' day.
Massa is a hansome man,
    Fine time o' day.
Massa is a dandy man,
    Fine time o' day.
Him hab de dollar, plenty too,
    Fine time o' day.

> Massa lub' a pretty girl,
> *Fine time o' day.*
> Him lub 'em much, him lub 'em true,
> *Fine time o' day.*
> Him hunt 'em round de guaba bush,
> *Fine time o' day.*
> Him catch 'em in de cane piece,
> *Fine time o' day, &c.*[15]

Throughout the nineteenth century, the English travelers witnessed such scenes as this one and noted them in their journals. Though there are few references to West Indian shantying on the open seas, these work episodes on shore continued to fascinate. One notable reporting is by Charles Kingsley, the author of *Westward Ho!* Kingsley, on a Christmas cruise to the West Indies, got his first taste of the sights and sounds of the region when his ship pulled up to the docks in St. Thomas.

Already a coal-barge lay on either side of her, and over the coals we scrambled, through a scene which we would fain forget. Black women on one side were doing men's work, with heavy coal-baskets on their head, amid screaming, chattering and language of which, happily, we understood little or nothing. On the other, a gang of men and boys, who as night fell, worked, many of them, altogether naked, their glossy bronze figures gleaming in the red lamp-light, and both men and women singing over their work in wild choruses, which when the screaming cracked voices of the women were silent, and the really rich tenors of the men had it to themselves, were not unpleasant. A lad, seeming the poet of the gang, stood on the sponson, and in the momentary intervals of work, improvised some story, while the men below took up and finished each verse with a refrain, piercing, sad,

---

[15] Wentworth, II, 240–242. The song is obviously directed as a song of derision at the white man transcribing the song, as it is a scandal piece of a fairly common sort about a white planter and his amorous attentions on the black women in St. Thomas. Though the song is unreported in Hugill, the refrain is still sung throughout the West Indies.

running up and down large and easy intervals. The tunes were many and seeming familiar, all barbaric, often ending in the minor key, and remind us much, perhaps too much, of the old Gregorian tones. The words were all but unintelligible. In one song we caught "New York" again and again, and the "Captain he heard it, he was troubled in his mind." "Ya-ha-he-ho-o-hu"—followed the chorus.

> "Captain he go to him cabin, he drink wine
>   and whiskey—"
> "Ya-he" &c.
> "You go to America? You as well go to heaven."
> "Ya-he" &c.[16]

A later reporting comes from James McQuade in *The Cruise of the Montauk*, who says that the following song was learned in the West Indies:

> We're bound for the West Indies straight,
>   Largy—Kargy, Haul away O—h.
> Come lively, boys, or we'll be late,
>   Weeny—Kreeny, Haul away O—h.
>
> We'll have rum and baccy plenty,
>   Largy—etc.
> Cocos, yams and argy-denty; [Aguardiente]
>   Weeny—etc. [corned beef]
>
> No more horse and dandy funky; [a mess of old biscuits
>   and molasses]
> But St. Kitten's roasted monkey.
>
> We'll go fiddle with black Peter.
> Dance all night with Wanneretter. [Juanita]
>
> At Kooreso [Curacao] we'll get frisky,
> Throwing dice with Dutch Francisky.
>
> When we've found the pirate's money,
> We'll live on shore eating honey.

[16] Charles Kingsley, *At Last: A Christmas in the West Indies*, pp. 20–21.

Wear big boots of allygator,
Taking Nance to the thayayter.

We'll bunk no more with cockroaches,
  Largy—Kargy, Haul away O—h,
But ride all day in soft coaches,
  Weeny—Kreeny, Haul away O—h.[17]

Of note in these reportings is that the travelers associated these songs not so much with deep-sea experiences as with a wide range of shore jobs—hauling coal, rowing boats, and various activities on the plantations. Though many of the songs reported are obviously related to ones used for sailing shanties, the fact is that these songs and others of their type have remained part of the on-shore repertoire for a wide number of employments and entertainments.

---

[17] James McQuade, *The Cruise of the Montauk*, p. 103. "St. Kitten's monkey" was the delicacy of the island of St. Kitts, so much so that they are now extinct. The author notes that the refrain probably refers to *largo cargo* (big cargo) and *buena carina* (good little girl).

2. *"Row, Bully, Row Boy"*

SINGING THE FISHING ON NEVIS AND TOBAGO

$\mathcal{T}$he persistence of shanties from the Anglo-American repertoire from one West Indian island to another seems to depend upon whether the island was one of those visited by the whalers or by large sailing ships on a regular basis: on such islands the ships would hire crew that would later return home and use the songs of the sea in the more usual insular occupations. We can thereby compare the repertoire of two fishing communities. One of these communities is in the British Leeward Islands, an area constantly visited by ships that were in search of the big whales or that came to haul away the molasses and rum produced by the fortune-making sugar industry. The other is on Tobago, which is below the British Windwards and far off the main-traveled routes for such ships (which would harbor in Trinidad, if they came to the area at all). The fishing operation, the trade in which shantying most often arises in both communities, is pursued through very much the same techniques. However, the repertoire of the Nevis fisher people is heavily reliant on songs from the international song stock, while Tobagonians seem to have their own local traditions that they use for the same purposes.

On both islands, shantying related to fishing has recently gone into a decline but for different reasons. On Nevis, the latest of many migrations (this time to the neighboring American Virgin Islands) has decimated the fishing communities. I first collected from the shanty singers in Newcastle, a fishing community on the Windward coast, in the summer of 1963. At that time there were a number of good shanty-men there. When I went back in 1966 all but one had departed, and he was the fisherman with the least initiative and the greatest unreliability. Furthermore, "Pops" Pemberton, the shanty-man from Charlestown, the metropolitan center of the island, had similarly departed in pursuit of higher wages and more reliable income. One man who had been a member of the Newcastle group happened to come for a visit during our sojourn in 1966 and reported that he had been able to get a job as captain on an inter-island cargo boat between the smaller Virgin Islands. He said that he was making $200 B.W.I. (approximately $100 U.S.) a month there and sending home half of that. He was fortunate if he earned $75 B.W.I. a month at fishing— the weekly wage paid by the government then being $7.50 for men and $4.50 for women.

The situation on Tobago is quite different. The *fisheners* as they called themselves in Plymouth (the town in which I lived for five months in winter, 1966–1967) were happy with their life, which permitted them a good income, and few of them were tempted to leave for greener pastures. In fact, those who went *fishenin'* on the reefs in their small boats had found such a market for their catch that they were able—often with the help of government loans—to get an outboard motor. Since most of their shanty singing had been accompaniment to their concerted rowing, the need for this type of singing had been fading. Yet the values surrounding this cooperative, expressive activity are still present and are discussed constantly.

Life in Plymouth comes very close to the ideal carrying-out of the extended-family system. The land and the sea are so productive that few fear an inability to feed their family. Land has been relatively

easy to purchase for the black inhabitants (as opposed to the situation
on most other islands of this size in the British West Indies), primarily
because the island was colonized late in the history of the area and
the plantation system was never very successful; a land-use system
emerged, *metayage*, which was something like share-cropping except
that it often embodied an understanding that the land might be pur-
chased by those working it. This tendency has been furthered by the
Trinidad and Tobago government's policies on land use, which force
absentee landlords to sell or develop; this policy has been imple-
mented by low-interest government loans available to those willing
to work the land themselves.

In addition to productive land, the fishing trade provides a living
for over half the town's men and a number of the women. Thus, there
are fewer who need to keep *gardens* (produce plots) in order to feed
their families, and a reasonable work alternative is presented for the
young men of the town. This situation often leads to members of a
family or close friends sharing out the products of their endeavors;
each night everyone will commonly have some *provisions* (vegetables,
usually starchy ones) and some fish for the pots.

This cooperative spirit is characteristic of the community and is
discussed a good deal in such terms. It is almost always talked about
in terms of how the community must operate as a big family; so their
own folk rationalization for the sharing procedures is based on the
analogy of the family.

Indeed, any kind of endeavor calling for personal interaction is
commonly regulated in familistic terms. The family is conceived of
in broad terms, and any kind of familiar relationship calls for an
acceptance of rights and obligations. Cousinship, thus, is calculated
for at least five degrees (i.e., to fifth cousin or to third cousin twice
removed), and even beyond that someone may be referred to as
"family" (as in " 'e family to me"). The importance of the family
designation becomes evident in walking down a street with a Plym-
outhian, for each person one passes is greeted with a term of rela-

tionship ("Good evening, cousin," "Goodnight, uncle"); or a remark is made, such as "she is family to me—I must call she 'Aunt.' " When a community squabble arises, which happens often, the discussion of it often turns on how the contestants are related to each other and therefore should not treat each other so.

The importance of family connection is further demonstrated by the institution of godparents. Each person commonly has two godparents of each sex, and they are greeted by this term of relationship as well. This relationship is intended to extend the family and incorporate non-blood relations, for all the other children of the same generation call the godparents of one "godfather" or "godmother," and the term is one of great respect.

The family concept acts as an agency of control in the community and brings about a certain amount of stability under the most trying situations. This stability becomes evident in crisis times, during sickness, after death, after childbirth, for a wedding, and so on. On any of these occasions, but especially after a death, the family coheres and works in a stylized cooperative way. Each member of the family, as well as members of the friendship network, performs some job associated with the interment, either baking and cooking, cutting the tree and making the coffin, or digging the grave.

This familistic frame of reference is even more noticeable in the personalization of each physical object introduced into the life of the family and the consequent treatment of this object in familiar ritualistic manner. Each boat, house, seine, or piece of land is baptized by the Anglican priest, and in the case of a boat or a seine by the godparents. Furthermore, as part of the ceremony, there is a sprinkling of many different kinds of waters (blood, rum, sugar water, etc.) on the object as a devotion to the ancestors.

The ancestors are regarded in a strange manner, for they are not feared (as in so many other West Indian groups who fear *jumbies* [the walking dead] and other such spirits). Rather, they are venerated as benevolent beings because that is how one's grandparents acted, and one loved one's grandparents. There is, however, no fear that a lack of respect would incur the wrath of the dead and the visitation of a *jumbie*.

These familistic conceptions are important to our present purpose, for interpersonal obligations, in line with the close family ties, are taken very seriously. Thus, there is a high degree of cooperative activity and a constant discussion of the importance of cooperation, especially when the joint enterprise is being threatened. The most extreme and formalized of such cooperative activities in Plymouth is life on the beach.

There are two kinds of fishing activities, drop-lining and seining. Drop-lining is done by those in the community who like to work individually, commonly ones who wish to marry early and escape the domination of their familial home (which in Plymouth is usually father-centered). This kind of fishing is done in one- or two-man boats on the reef and involves catching the large fish that are very popular in the markets. Drop-lining is often done at night with the aid of large lanterns, or *flambeaus*.

Seining, on the other hand, is done on the beach and during the day. This activity is directed more toward catching the schools of small fish that come closer to shore—the jacks, robins, and sprats that may be caught by the thousands when a run is on. Seining takes a good deal of cooperation in order for it to be successful. The nets are thrown by crews of six, and each man on the beach commonly belongs to one (or more) crews. The seine is taken into the bay by a center-boat and cast into the water about 100 to 150 feet offshore. The ends of the seine are then taken by two of the *fisheners* who then jump into the water, carrying them to the shore at points about fifty to seventy-five feet apart. At this point, others join them, and everyone on the beach helps to pull the seines in.

There are commonly eleven to thirteen seines on the beach, and, because of the size of the beach, only two can be cast at a time. The crews, therefore, have to wait their turn, or, as it is called in Plymouth, their *share*. This means that a seine will be thrown until a good catch is made, which may take as long as a week, though usually it is one day or less. The others must wait. Because everyone helps pull in the seine, it is virtually guaranteed that everyone will have some *piece of fish* for his pot that night, for even a bad haul will catch something. Furthermore, there is often an arrangement, arising from family ties, that those fishermen who catch by drop-lining will share with some beach *fisheners* on the bad days, expecting to be repaid in kind on the numerous occasions when their forays come to naught. Friendship and family are most commonly demonstrated by the giving of fish in exchange for provisions from the agrarian sector of the community or for fish from other *fisheners*.

The idea of beach seining, however, goes beyond providing fish for the pots of the community. The possibility always exists for making the big catch, which will then be marketed by trucks throughout the island, the fish selling for what the traffic will bear. (On the occasion of one enormous catch, we saw the price go from 20¢ a pound to a truckload of fish being thrown into the sea on the other side of the island because of a saturation of the market and an overexposure of the fish to the sun.) The fish, except on the occasions of these huge catches, are sold to women vendors (often family) who sell them in the market of the capital, Scarborough, for twice the beach price. This price difference sometimes leads to hard feelings on the part of the *fisheners*.

On days in which early net castings are not good, there is a tendency to wait a few hours before casting again. The early morning and the evening are the times of greatest activity. Along with the system of *shares*, there are great stretches of time for leisure in which the men *lime* on the beach. *Liming* is the West Indian term for sitting around, talking and eating and drinking rum; on the beach *liming* is accompanied by the men working to repair each others' seines and accompanying equipment. Each crew is primarily responsible for its own maintenance and is therefore governed by the *captain* of the crew; but commonly anyone around will help in repairing the seines, which are constantly being torn by the rocks on the bottom of the bay.

This cooperative attitude is extended to the *knitting* or *tying* of new seines. In Plymouth, as opposed to most other parts of the island, it is not necessary to pay for help in making a seine, since all the good knitters (always men) will volunteer or be asked. A certain amount of prestige is involved in being a part of such an endeavor, for I've seen men in a pique for not being asked to knit and seine owners vexed because someone they call friend had either not offered to help or had done so and failed to perform as quickly as expected.

In many ways, then, Plymouthians attempt to live up to the highest ideals of the extended-family system—cooperation based on respect, respect in turn arising from one's age and assumption of familial responsibility. There are, of course, constant breakdowns in the system. Many forces, coming mainly from sources outside the community, have brought about dissension. Furthermore, fights within families occur constantly, most often between a parent and a child, the weakest spot in an extended-family system in which age is equated with power and authority. But such problems are taken care of, either through the constabulary and the courts (a very common recourse in family arguments) or through the departure of the younger person to Scarborough or Trinidad. In this way, the young people with the greatest amount of drive and initiative or with the greatest amount of hostility (the two often go together) have a place to go to, also relieving the town of their disruptive presence. Outlets of this sort have also provided a leveling feature on the population and thus preserved the cooperative endeavor I am talking about.

But there are enough of these motives, even in beach life, to create factions and long-standing antagonisms and occasional outbursts of hostility. For instance, when a large catch is made by a seining crew and it is obvious that a school is running, the whole system of the beach breaks down, and the first boat out gets to throw first; arguments and physical fights often result. But these are not at all usual.

More common are the hostilities that arise when the fish are not running very often and the crews therefore have to wait for a long time before their *chance* comes up. Fights on the beach are much more frequent then, and fewer men bother to go there. One release from these tensions occurs with one of the crews leaving with its boat and seine to another less populated beach on the island. On such occasions the shanties are used.

Much singing goes on on the beach in the normal round of affairs, for singing is part of *liming*. What is unusual is that the coordinating work songs are not an adjunct of the seine-pulling ceremony, for virtually every other community activity has singing, and its most common form is the chanter-response pattern. Characteristic of this chanter-response pattern are the numerous songs sung at *bongo* wakes, dance songs in which a singer leads and the rest join in the chorus, while dancing. It is also true of the songs sung on the beach on *Fishermen's Fête*, St. Peter's Day, June 29. At that time, each of the beach singers feels that he must make up a song for the visiting fishermen who come from all over the island. They commonly sing of the beauties of the fête, using a traditional tune but introducing topical subjects and an appropriate chorus line. Here is a pattern, for instance, which was improvised upon by one of the singers the year before we lived in Plymouth.

> St. Peter, St. Peter, down at Courland Bay,[1]
> St. Peter, St. Peter, St. Peter, Courland Bay.
>
> And the water is very fresh and feel fresh and gay,
> St. Peter, St. Peter, down at Courland Bay.
>
> Oh, darling, I'm going to St. Peter's Day,
> St. Peter, St. Peter, St. Peter, Courland Bay.
>
> Fishermen get toegther on St. Peter's Day,
> St. Peter, St. Peter, St. Peter, Courland Bay.

[1] The local seining bay; pronounced Cōlonbay.

"St. Peter Down at Courland Bay"

Darling do do I'm going to St. Peter's Day,
St. Peter, St. Peter, St. Peter, Courland Bay.

Oh, we're going to drink and be merry on that day,
St. Peter, St. Peter, St. Peter, Courland Bay.

Darling do do I'm takin' you with me,
St. Peter, St. Peter, St. Peter, Courland Bay.

Etc., *ad lib.*

Singing and dancing in a group are the prevalent forms of ceremonial entertainment in the community.[2] Songs that are used for one occasion tend to crop up in other settings. The group may derive songs from local traditions, from Trinidad, from something heard on the radio, or from any source that allows them to put it in their own style. Consequently, there are few songs that are thought of by the men as shanties alone. That there used to be something of a corpus of shanties is indicated by the few songs that are sung by the men when they encounter difficulty in rowing while they are off on these jaunts to another beach. Furthermore, I had a number of discussions with the men on the beach; on one occasion an older man, Latchford John, who had never been a fisherman, said that there had been a number of special work songs, and he was able to recall one that others agreed they had heard in much use. This song was the unusual "Monkey Married the Baboon's Daughter," which derives in part from a popular music hall song of the nineteenth century (indicating that the practice of deriving songs from various sources was of some duration in the community).

> Oh, what a hell a wedding over Congo River,
> Wo, ho, ho, me bully boy.
>
> Monkey married to baboon' daughter,
> Wo, ho, ho, me bully boy.
>
> What do you t'ink dey had for dere dinner?
> Mosquito gall and a sandfly liver,
> Wo, ho, ho, me bully.
>
> The father fish went to stake de key,
> Baboon say he might cake alone,
> At lunch he get up to shade de rice,
> Monkey say, "Leave de rice alone."
> Wo, ho, ho, me bully boy.

[2] In fact, as I have discussed earlier other patterns of performance have been rejected (Roger Abrahams, "Public Drama in Two West Indian Islands," *Trans-Action*, June–July 1968).

"Oh, What a Hell of a Wedding"

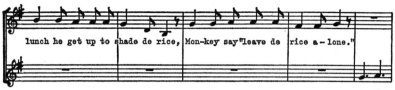

lunch he get up to shade de rice, | Mon-key say "leave de | rice a – lone."

Wo, ho,

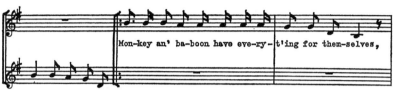

Mon-key an' ba-boon have eve-ry – | t'ing for them-selves,

ho, me bul-ly boy.

Repeat 2 bar phrase
and 2 bar refrain
to end, ad lib

Wo, ho, ho, me bul – ly boy.

Monkey an' baboon have everyt'ing for themselves,
Wo, ho, ho, me bully boy.

Gonna have the biggest wedding over Congo River,
Wo, ho, ho, me bully boy.

Monkey married to baboon' daughter,
Wo, ho, ho, me bully boy.

Everyt'ing in the feas' he had,
Wo, ho, ho, me bully boy.

Monkey and baboon take all for themselves,
Wo, ho, ho, me bully boy.

Nobody take a tas'e from them,
Wo, ho, ho, me bully boy.

Monkey and baboon they na share whe they have,
Wo, ho, ho, me bully boy.[3]

As noted, there is one experience that calls forth traditional shanties—the encountering of strong winds and tides while rowing. All the songs sung for this purpose are close to the international type of shanty, but they have a content that comments on the problems encountered by the *fisheners* who are rowing. The first of these songs that were reported to me was "Michael (or Jonah), Row the Boat Ashore," sung to the same tune in which it was popular in the United States, but with very different words.

"Michael, Row the Boat Ashore"

Michael, row the boat ashore,
Hallelujah;
Michael, row the boat ashore,
Hallelujah.

[3] It is interesting to note the topic of this song, given the high value placed on sharing. Latchford was a bit of a pariah in the community because of his selfish tendencies. Furthermore, he told many Anansi stories about the spider's voracious appetites in which Anansi tricked others out of their food sources.

Michael, row the boat ashore,
Hallelujah;
Oh, the current is from the north to the wes',
Hallelujah.

Fisherman day is very cold,
Hallelujah;
Michael, haul the boat ashore,
Hallelujah.

Oh, Michael, go and gone too late,
Hallelujah;
De current is going from north to south,
Hallelujah.

Michael, row the boat ashore,
Hallelujah;
Long day hard, but very soon,
Hallelujah.

Michael, take the boat ashore,
Hallelujah;
Michael, haul, we go ashore,
Hallelujah.

Fisherman day is very hard,
Hallelujah;
Tidal wave is coming too,
Hallelujah.

Naturally I was taken aback by the elicitation of this song, so I asked the singers where they had learned it. This led to assertions that they had sung the song long before they had heard it on the radio (but then they claimed the same for other songs they could not have learned in any other way since they were recent popular compositions). However, the discussion immediately led, without any prodding, to a consideration of why they sang sometimes "Michael," sometimes "Jonah." The answer, given by Isaac Williams, a middle-aged *fishener* and seine owner, was:

*We use this song when we lef' from home and the tide is very hard,
and we turn back home, and we star' to row de boat. So the captain
of the boat sing that song, an' we answer the chorus. Keep us lively
to row.*

*We sing Michael or Jonah or anybody' name. Captain of the boat is
Michael so he singing that for the crew, so, to encourage. You understand. For when the current is very hard there, we fear it a lot and
have someone to gi' it courage to take the boat ashore, otherwise. . . .
So we sing that song to encourage the boys.*

*In a boat and in these difficulties, the captain, he the lasten one to
give up hopes. He have to 'courage his men. He can' be a coward, although he be a cowardly man he can' show it out. Nah, nah. He have
to be the las' to [leave the ship]. So then I believe in those days, 'e bus'
[burst] that song on 'e crews to give them fait', an' they no believe 'e
have fait'. Well 'e sung that song, "Michael Row the Boat Ashore,"
and sing chorus with him. And every crew in that boat has look back,
see where we have a brave captain and we also ha' to be brave. The
las' man in a boat or a ship is the captain, for to encourage his crew.*

Another such song, traditionally used while rowing, is "Pull Away Me
Boy." As with all the other songs, the subject is announced and there
are a few set stanzas that are repeated *ad lib.*

> Pull away me boy,
> Pull away me boy.
>
> An' 'e eat all me money,
> Pull away me boy.
>
> An' 'e nyam[4] all me money,
> Pull away me boy.
>
> Pull away, pull away,
> Pull away me boy.
>
> An' 'e bawl "qua qua qua qua,"
> Pull away me boy.

[4] Also means "eat."

"Pull Away Me Boy"

All other verses are variations of one of the previous five 2-bar phrases, which may or may not be repeated.

And you hear me say,
Pull away me boy.

Do you hear-a wha' me say?
Pull away me boy.

And you do wha' me tell you,
Pull away me boy.

And you go where me go,
Pull away me boy.

And you pull as we go,
Pull away me boy.

An' you come, le' we go,
Pull away me boy.

Bombo nyam all me money,
Pull away me boy.

Pull way me lover,
Pull away me boy.

You see, I'm going to tell you. At leas' we 'quaint you wid it. Well the fishermen go and toil job hard, and when they come back they meet a lot a woman on the beach. Y' understand? And they have a, as you call, a sex. So we broke it up in that verse, we call it "bombo." We came on shore with the fish an' we sell it an' woman was on de beach and we went an' have sex wid dem an' dey take all the cash becau' they come work an' get there no money. So we call that "bombo."

Another song that continues to be used in the rowing operation is "Man-o-War Sailor." This song probably refers not to one who shipped on a man-of-war but to a fisherman from Man-O-War Bay (near Charlotteville), Tobago.

Man-o-war sailor, you better le' me go;
Man-o-war sailor, ho-heave-ho.

Man-o-war sailor, I'm trying to go home;
Man-o-war sailor, ho-heave-ho.

"Man-o-War Sailor"

Man-o-war sailor, I'm going home;
Man-o-war sailor, ho-heave-ho.

Man-o-war sailor, I'm rowing home;
Man-o-war sailor, ho-heave-ho.

Man-o-war sailor, the current going home;
Man-o-war sailor, ho-heave-ho.

Etc., *ad lib.*

In many ways, life in Newcastle, Nevis, is as different from that of Plymouth as one can imagine in two communities within the same culture areas and having such similar historical and geographic features. For just as Tobago serves something as a satellite to Trinidad and is therefore much less populated and mechanized, so is Nevis related to St. Kitts. But whereas cooperation and other such familiar agrarian values are the dominating focus for interpersonal life style at Plymouth, on Nevis mistrust and competition rule. Tobagonians seem to love each other and the life on their island, while Nevisians and especially Newcastlers trust no one and look for any excuse whatsoever to escape the island.

As one of the Mother Colonies, Nevis has been heavily populated since the early seventeenth century and has remained so ever since, in spite of frequent migrations. Furthermore, the land was overtilled during the era of great fortunes and is now unproductive; yet, in contrast to Tobago, it has remained in the hands of a few, often absentee, landowners. Consequently, wresting a living of any sort has been extremely difficult and has led to a highly competitive expectation of life. Consequently, Nevisian folklore has a distinctly paranoid cast to it, preaching in its proverbs and songs the necessity of watching the other person all the time lest one be taken advantage of.

This situation is reflected in the way fishing is done in the area. Though the beaches are ideal for seining, since there are few rocks to snag the net and ample schools to fill the nets from time to time, such uses are not permitted since the beaches are privately owned. There is, however, no pressure to allow more seines, for the cooperative activity needed to pull the seine in is difficult to bring about. Not enough people are on the beaches, except in Charlestown itself; a seine is thrown there about once a day.

Paralleling these Nevisian attitudes is the style of fishing—the use of pots (or traps) that are placed in constantly changing spots by individual boats and left to gather the smaller fish and langouste lobsters found on the floor of the lagoon and on the inner and outer edges of the reef. An attempt is made to keep the placement of the pots secret because the catch might otherwise be stolen. Such boats commonly take a crew of up to four, though one may take a craft out by oneself if necessary. There is a ready market for the catch on Nevis, though it is often carried over to Basseterre, St. Kitts, where prices are slightly higher. The fish are commonly sold from the boat or, in the case of remarkable catches, to a cab driver or another man on the beach who takes his basket in his car; blowing on his conch-horn, he sells at the crossroads where the buyers congregate with plate in hand to carry home the purchase.

Shantying, since it rests on cooperative activity, would seem to be an anathema to such a life view. However, there are certain activities which the men have not learned to perform by themselves. One of these, mentioned in the first chapter, is housemoving, a constant necessity on the island; whenever a great fight occurs between neighbors, one of them often finds it more convenient and comfortable to move his house away along with his family. With the growth of truck ownership on the island, however, the necessity for a group of men to haul a house a long distance no longer arises very often. Now, instead of the longer hauling shanties, one simply hears the big lift routines, such as the shanty on pages 4–6 or the chanted

> The ram, the ewe, the wether;
> We all must lift together!

This rhyme is also used for another of the still-necessary cooperative activities—taking the boats from the water before hurricane season and putting them back in the sea afterward. Hurricane season, as explained by the West Indian, is known by the mnemonic

> June—too soon;
> July—stand by;
> August—you must;
> September—remember;
> October—all over.

By the first of July all the boats are out of the water. Until recently this job was done by getting all the men down on the beach to help by providing them with plenty of rum; the owner also hired a drummer (usually a *big drum*, which is bamboo fife, trap and bass drums

both being played with sticks in the European manner) to come to
the beach and play as an encouragement to the workers. The most
common of the hauling shanties is directed at the drummer, making
fun of him.

"Caesar Boy, Caesar"

Caesar drummer want paper drum,
Caesar boy, Caesar.
Caesar drummer want paper drum,
Caesar boy, Caesar.

Oh, Caesar drummer want paper drum,
Caesar boy, Caesar.
Oh, you look on Caesar, you no look on me,
Caesar boy, Caesar.

Oh, Caesar drummer want kettle drum,
Caesar boy, Caesar.
Oh, Caesar drummer want kettle drum,
Caesar boy, Caesar.

Oh, you look on Caesar, you no look on me,
Caesar boy, Caesar.

Oh, you look on Caesar, you no look on me,
Caesar boy, Caesar.

Oh, Caesar drummer want paper drum,
Caesar boy, Caesar.
Oh, Caesar drummer want paper drum,
Caesar boy, Caesar.

Oh, you look on Caesar, you no look on me,
Caesar boy, Caesar.
Oh, you look on Caesar, you no look on me,
Caesar boy, Caesar.

Oh, Caesar drummer go boom, boom, boom,
Caesar boy, Caesar.
Oh, Caesar drummer go boom, boom, boom,
Caesar boy, Caesar.

Etc., *ad lib.*

Another shanty for the purpose of pushing and lifting either a boat or a house describes the operation, with the usual encouragements.

"Shub Her Down"

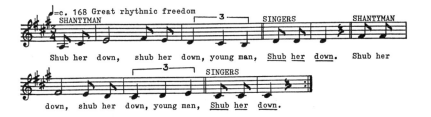

Shub her down, shub her down, young man,
Shub her down.
Shub her down, shub her down, young man,
Shub her down.

Wheel away, wheel away, young man,
Wheel away.
Wheel away, wheel away, out there,
Wheel away.

Shub her out, shub her out, I say,
Shub her out.
Shub her out, shub her out, I say,
Shub her out.

Long and strong, long and strong, young man,
Long and strong.
Long and strong, long and strong, young man,
Long and strong.

Wheel away, wheel away, young man,
Wheel away.
Wheel away, wheel away, out there,
Wheel away.

We can do it, we can do it, I say,
We can do it.
Long and strong, long and strong, young man,
Long and strong.

Etc., *ad lib.*

Another one concerned with lifting and shoving that also describes the rigors of such activity is "Georgy." The pace of this shanty indicates that it is associated with the part of the job when a number of quick, short lifts are needed.

Georgy, me neck-a-broke
Hold 'em George, I damn near neck-a-broke;
Hold 'em George, I damn near are too broke;
Hold 'em George, I got no neck-a-broke.

Georgy, me neck-a-broke
Hold 'em George, I damn near are too broke;

Hold 'em George, I got no neck-a-broke;
Hold 'em George, I damn near neck-a-broke.

Etc., *ad lib.*

"Georgy, Me Neck-a-Broke"

These pushing shanties are the ones most commonly used, and they come from local tradition for the most part. In contrast to these are the rowing shanties used in the past on Nevis, which are primarily from the repertoire of the deep-sea sailor.

> When it's cyam [calm] when we're on the ocean, we sing de shan-ties. Yah—It helps, the singing. It helps the pulling—pull de boat. You see when we sing together, we move together. We move de oars together when we pulling. Yes. It makes it mo' easier—because we sing together and we row together, we find it mo' easier in so doing.

The boats are equipped with one large sail which is sloop-rigged and regulated not only by the usual manipulation of the position and tension of the sail but also by pulling the sail up or letting it down very quickly or by both methods together. Maneuvering is dangerous for the 'Castle fisherman since he must constantly contend with cross-

ing a reef and with contrary winds that blow in the pass between
Nevis and the St. Kitts peninsula, about a mile and a half away. Part
of the contrariety of the winds is that a calm can set in within a matter of minutes, especially in the middle of the day. It is at these times
that the rowing occurs. I should note that of all the times I waited on
the beach for fish or lobsters at 'Castle, I never heard any shanties
being sung; so it seems that the following shanties were survivals
rather than functional work songs, a fact borne out by the reports of
my singers.

Nonetheless, the repertoire is an interesting one when considering
West Indian shantying traditions since it betrays a heavy reliance on
the Anglo-American song repertoire. However, at least two of these
widely collected songs have been accounted for as West Indian in
origin, "Long Time Ago" and "Fire Down Below." The latter is represented by two possible versions, the second being at least
thematically related.

"Long Time Ago"

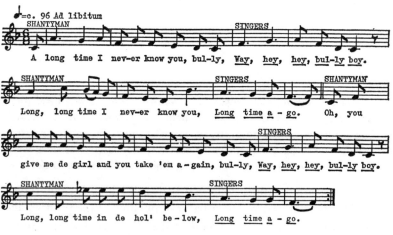

A long time I never know you, bully,
Way, hey, hey, bully boy.

Long, long time I never know you,
Long time ago.

Oh, you give me de girl and you take 'em again, bully,
Way, hey, hey, bully boy.
Long, long time in de hol' below,
Long time ago.

Oh, a long, long time I never know you, bully,
Way, hey, hey, bully boy.
Long, long time in de hol' below,
Long time ago.

Oh, you give me de girl and you take 'em again, bully,
Way, hey, hey, bully boy.
Long, long time in de hol' below,
Long time ago.

Oh, what long, long time I never hear you, bully,
Way, hey, hey, bully boy.
Long, long time in de hol' below,
Long time ago.

Etc., *ad lib.*

"Fire Down Below"

Send to call the wa-ter man,

Fire down be-low.

Below, below me boy,
Fire down below.
Below, below me boy,
Fire down below.

Oh, fire in the main arch,
Fire down below.
Send to call de water man,
Fire down below.

Oh, send to call de water man,
Fire down below.
Oh, fire in the main arch,
Fire down below.

Oh, fire in the main hol',
Fire down below.
Oh, fire in the main hol',
Fire down below.

Oh, fire in the main arch,
Fire down below.
Send for, call de captain,
Fire down below.

Oh, fire in the main hol',
Fire down below.
Oh, fire in the arch hol',
Fire down below.

Oh, fire in the arch hol',
Fire down below.

Below, below, below, below,
Fire down below.

Etc., *ad lib.*

"John, John, the Water Man"

I went down to Gila Point,
To hear master Sheila blow,

John, John, de water man,
The fire man below, boy,
John, John, de water man,
John, John, de oh.

Break oar, break oar,
Me master can' buy more,
John, John, de water man,
John, John, below,
Singing John, John, de water man,
John, John, below.

I stepped right up to Gila,
To hear master Sheila blow,
John, John, de water man,
The fire down below, boy,
Singing John, John, the water man,
John, John, below.

Broke oar, broke oar,
Me master can' buy more,
John, John, de water man,
The fire down below, boy,
Singing John, John, de water man,
John, John, below.

This song purports to describe the burning of a boat a long time ago off a point on St. Kitts; the sailors seemed to be lamenting the owner's inability to buy another boat. The singers thought Sheila referred to the wind.

Many shanty collectors have commented about the obscenities usually contained in these songs of men. Once, while collecting in Newcastle, the men began singing a song that began " 'Castle girls have dirty bloomers," and the women within hearing wouldn't allow the singing to proceed. However, the next song that came along was the following, which they enjoyed heartily.

"Woman Belly Full o' Hair"

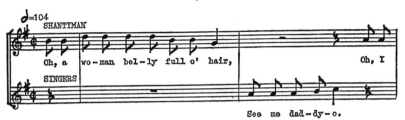

Oh, a woman belly full o' hair,
See me daddy-o.
Oh, I see it when I went in there,
See me daddy-o.

Oh, a woman belly full o' hair,
See me daddy-o.
Oh, hurrah for de golden,
See me daddy-o.

If you want to see a monkey dance,
See me daddy-o.
Broke a pepper in 'e ass,
See me daddy-o.

Woman belly full o' hair,
See me daddy-o.
Hurrah for de golden,
See me daddy-o.

If you want to see a monkey trick,
See me daddy-o.
Broke a pepper 'pon the prick,
See me daddy-o.

Woman belly full o' hair,
See me daddy-o.
Hurrah for the golden,
See me daddy-o.

Etc., *ad lib.*

Another song one might consider obscene is directed at East Indians and their purported tendency toward incestuous acts. This song does not reflect a real social situation on Nevis, since there were only three East Indian families, none of whom were ever discussed in such stereotyped terms.

"A Coolie Is Nobody"

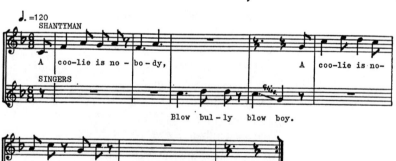

A coolie is nobody,
Blow bully blow boy.
A coolie is nobody, bully,
Blow (my) bully boy, blow.

But I never jumped your mommy,
Blow bully blow boy.
Never jumped your mommy, bully,
Blow (my) bully boy, blow.

They call me bully hangman,
Blow bully blow boy.
Never hanged your mommy, bully,
Blow (my) bully boy, blow.

Oh, a coolie is nobody,
Blow bully blow boy.
A coolie is nobody, bully,
Blow (my) bully boy, blow.

They call me bully jumper,
Blow bully blow boy.
Never jumped your mommy, bully,
Blow (my) bully boy, blow.

A coolie is nobody,
Blow bully blow boy.
Blow my bully, and blow my bully,
Blow (my) bully boy, blow.

Oh, a coolie is nobody,
Blow bully blow boy.
I never jumped your mommy, bully,
Blow (my) bully boy, blow.

Etc., *ad lib.*

John Gould, in the following song, is supposed by the men to have been a shipowner who lost his cargo.

"Bear Away Yankee, Bear Away Boy"

Oh, deep de water and shallow de shore,
Bear away Yankee, bear away boy.
Bear away an' dere she go,
Bear away Yankee, bear away boy.

Oh, deep de water and shallow de shore,
Bear away Yankee, bear away boy.

Bear away to Noble Bay,
Bear away Yankee, bear away boy.

Oh, what me going tell John Gould today?
Bear away Yankee, bear away boy.
What me going tell John Gould today?
Bear away Yankee, bear away boy.

Oh, what me going tell John Gould today?
Bear away Yankee, bear away boy.
Deep de water, shallow a shore,
Bear away Yankee, bear away boy.

Bear away Yankee, bear away boy,
Bear away Yankee, bear away boy.
What me going tell John Gould today?
Bear away Yankee, bear away boy.

Etc., *ad lib.*

The ridiculous food in the next shanty occurs in comic routines, jokes, and tales throughout the West Indies, always eliciting great laughter from the audience.

Oh me, captain, captain, what for me dinner?
Blow boy blow.
Salt fish liver and white lice color,
Blow my bully boy blow.

Come blow today, come blow tomorrow,
Blow boy blow.
Oh, you blow, you blow, you blow, you blow,
Blow my bully boy blow.

Come blow today, come blow tomorrow,
Blow boy blow.
Come blow away, I long to hear you,
Blow my bully boy blow.

Oh, captain, captain, what for my dinner?
Blow boy blow.

"Blow Boy Blow"

Salt fish color and white lice liver,
Blow my bully boy blow.

Come blow today, come blow tomorrow,
Blow boy blow.
Oh, you blow, you blow, you blow, you blow,
Blow my bully boy blow.

Oh, captain, captain, what for my dinner?
Blow boy blow.
A tin-fish head and a white lice liver,
Blow my bully blow.

Oh, you blow today, you blow tomorrow,
Blow boy blow.

You blow away, I long to hear you,
Blow my bully boy blow.

Etc., *ad lib.*

In line with the Anglo-American sea song tradition, these Nevisians sang many songs about their women on shore—both their sweethearts and their whores. As usual, Judy, Susanna, and Liza are the heroines, but Sally Brown is found as Feeny, perhaps her original name, since she was from Bermuda according to most accounts.

"Judiano"

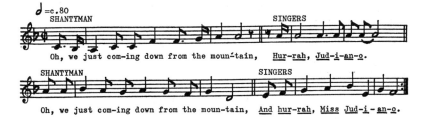

Oh, we just coming down from the mountain,
Hurrah, Judiano.
Oh, we just coming down from the mountain,
And hurrah, Miss Judiano.

Oh, the wife, oh, she had made out,[5]
Hurrah, Judiano.
Oh, the wife, well, she had made out,
And hurrah, Judiano.

Oh, me bottom belly a-burn me,
Hurrah, Judiano.
And me bottom belly a-burn me,
And hurrah, Judiano.

[5] Singer's explanation: she made out a bill!

"Oh, Louisiana"

Oh, the mountain so high and the valley so low,
Oh, Louisiana.
Louisiana, my darling, my Jane and Susanna,
We're bound right over the mountain.

Oh, the mountain so high and the valley so low,
Oh, Louisiana.
Louisiana, my darling, my Jane and Susanna,
We're bound right over the mountain.

"When You Go, Tell Julia (I Am Bound Away)"

♩=125

SHANTYMAN: Oh, when you go, tell Ju-li-a, SINGERS: I am bound a-way. SHANTYMAN: Oh, when you go, tell

SINGERS: Ju-li-a, I am bound a-way. SHANTYMAN: Oh, when you go, tell Ju-li-a, SINGERS: I am bound a-

SHANTYMAN: way. When you go, tell Ju-lia, SINGERS: Oh, I am bound a-way. SHANTYMAN: I'm bound a-way to

see the light, SINGERS: I am bound a-way. SHANTYMAN: I'm bound a-way to see my doc-ky,

SINGERS: I am bound a-way.

Oh, when you go, tell Julia,
I am bound away.
Oh, when you go, tell Julia,
I am bound away.

Oh, when you go, tell Julia,
I am bound away.
When you go, tell Julia,
Oh, I am bound away.

I'm bound away to see the light,
I am bound away.
I'm bound away to see my docky,
I am bound away.

I'm bound for North Carolina,
I am bound away.

I'm bound for North Carolina,
Oh, I am bound away.

Etc., *ad lib.*

Feeny Brown is the belle of Bermuda,
Ay yo, Feeny.
Feeny Brown is the belle of Bermuda,
Spend my money on Feeny Brown.[6]

Oh, give her a dollar she hol' for anodder,
Ay yo, Feeny.
Give her a dollar she hol' for anodder,
Spend my money on the girls ashore.

Feeny Brown is the belle of Bermuda,
Ay yo, Feeny.
Feeny Brown is the wordliest [?] mulatta,
Spend my money on the girls ashore.

Give her a dollar she hol' for anodder,
Ay yo, Feeny.
Give her a dollar she hol' for anodder,
Spend my money on the girls ashore.

Etc., *ad lib.*

"Feeny Brown"

[6] This is sung alternately "spending money on the girls ashore."

Fee-ny Brown is the belle of Ber-mu-da, Oh,

Spend my mo-ney on Fee-ny Brown.

give her a dol-lar she hol' for a-nod-der,

Ay yo, Fee-ny.

Give her a dol-lar she hol' for a - nod-der,

Spend my mo-ney on the

girls a - shore.

Finally, they sang a pair of songs that are among the most common in the deep-sea tradition, "Yankee John, Stormalong" and "Blow the Man Down."

> Oh, to me Liza Lane,
> Yankee John, Stormalong.
>
> Stormalong with the long boots on,
> Yankee John, Stormalong.

Oh, bully, night and day,
Yankee John, Stormalong.

Stormalong with the long boots on,
Yankee John, Stormalong.

Oh, to me Liza Lane,
Yankee John, Stormalong.

Stormalong with the long boots on,
Yankee John, Stormalong.

Stormalong, night and day.
Yankee John, Stormalong.

Oh, to me Liza Lane,
Yankee John, Stormalong.

Stormalong with the long boots on,
Yankee John, Stormalong.

"Yankee John, Stormalong"

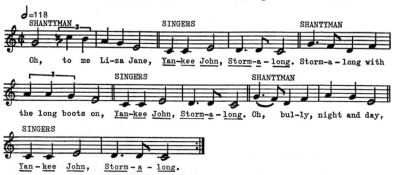

I hit him a lick and I fetch him a kick,
And a yea, yea, blow de man down.
Blow de man down in de hol' below,
'Low me some time to blow de man down.

Blow de man down and a blow de man down,
And a yea, yea, blow de man down.

"Blow the Man Down"

Hit him a lick and I fetch him a kick,
'Low me some time to blow de man down.

Blow de man down and a hit de man down,
And a yea, yea, blow de man down.
Blow de man down in de hol' below,
'Low me some time to blow de man down.

Etc., *ad lib.*

The Nevisian songs, as noted, are of interest in terms of what they tell us about the reciprocal relations between the Anglo-American and the West Indian shantying traditions. But, as a singing tradition unto itself, it betrays a poverty and sterility that becomes apparent when compared to the Tobago tradition, which seizes upon any group occasion to sing shanty-type songs. Even more dramatically rich, because they too derive from the Anglo-American repertoire, are the songs of the Barouallie, St. Vincent, whalers, which will be described next.

3. *"Solid Fas'"* Our Captain Cry Out

BLACKFISHING AT BAROUALLIE

$\mathcal{J}$n the great days of whaling in the nineteenth century, there were many places in the eastern Caribbean that served as way stations for the international whaling trade. This trade was of economic importance to West Indians, primarily because it provided wage employment for some who joined the crews of the whaling ships. As one West Indian writer observed of this situation:

> There is, or was, every year a large number of American whaling schooners visiting Dominica and St. Vincent, Grenada and other Islands, where the catch at times is very remunerative. At Dominica they lay in their stock of vegetables preparatory to cruising about. The boat hands are also recruited from young creoles of the different islands, as they all row well, and can stand exposure to the sun better than the Yankee.
>
> A good number of these lads continue in the vessels till they return to Massachusetts, and thence they ship for various parts. In time they come home, wonderfully improved by having had to work hard, and being under discipline. Food too of a better kind than the yam and salt fish of their native place has produced good results, and it is difficult to recognize in a strong muscular sailor well clad, the

owner of a huge pair of boots, and his speech strongly marked with
the Yankee accent, the thin-legged ragged, ill-nurtured lad, one's
boatman or fisherman of the previous year or so.[1]

A whaling voyage of just this variety is admirably described in
words and pictures in Robert Cushman Murphy's books, *A Logbook
for Grace* and *A Dead Whale or a Stove Boat*. A record of a whaling
trip in 1912–1913 with a crew made up in the main of West Indians,
these books describe just what day-to-day life was like on such runs.
Characteristic of such literature, as part of the description of the
whaling operation, was a discussion of the importance of shantying:

> Power plant. Under the Old Man's eye nearly half of *Daisy's* crew
> stands on the top gallant forecastle and rocks the windlass which takes
> up the rope. This runs first aloft to the cutting tackle and thence
> down to the blubber hook. It's toil but with rhythm.
>
> For this is the cheery part of the business; it swings to song. The
> Doctor (ship's cook), or a raucous officer bellows the verses of time-
> honored chanties—some of them very hairy chested—and all the
> sweating boys join in the chorus, whether "Whiskey Johnny," "Blow,
> blow, blow the man down!" or another.[2]

But it was not until rather late in the history of whaling that West
Indian communities arose in which the whale was hunted to provide
not only oil (and occasional ambergris) but also food for the island-
ers. Of these, only Barouallie, St. Vincent, and its neighboring communities on Bequia seem to be still pursuing the whales.

Barouallie is on the Leeward coast of St. Vincent, situated on a
magnificent bay, surrounded by high hills and cliffs on every side but
the sea. Its architecture and town plan still reflect the original French
settlement. Until recently the town was effectively isolated because
the road leading from Kingstown, the capital of the island, was so
bad. Trips to Kingstown were confined, for the most part, to the sea

---

[1] "X. Beke," *West Indian Yarns.*
[2] Robert Cushman Murphy, *A Dead Whale or a Stove Boat*, pp. 102–104.

access and for most residents were made only on Saturdays when the boats would have a race to see who could get to town first. Trips during the rest of the week would be only for selling meat or other commerce.

The town life of Barouallie revolves around its one industry, whaling for the "blackfish" (*Globecephalus melas*). Consequently, it regards its relationship with the other whaling community on the satellite island of Bequia in the Grenadines more deeply than its ties with Kingstown—a place that signifies in the minds of many the problems of exploitation. In point of fact, Barouallie's industry is an outgrowth of the Grenadines' whale fishing and so the felt relationship has important historical reasons. And the Barouallie men still use boats made on Bequia.

Whaling as a commercial venture, according to the local accounts, was brought into the area by a Scotsman named "Old Bill" Wallace in the 1880's or 1890's. Wallace came to the Grenadines in the seventies or early eighties and bought a plantation with his savings from whaling, only to find that venture a failure. He subsequently taught his new neighbors his trade, and the industry was begun. Frederic Fenger, who met him in 1912, noted of him:

> At the magical age of fifteen he had spewed the silver spoon from his mouth and left it on his hearth in his Scotland home to taste the first sting of remorse under the care of the Yankee skipper. He finally drifted to Bequia with his earnings and bought a large sugar plantation. But the seafaring man rarely prospers on land. The failure of cane sugar in the islands, followed by a disastrous hurricane, brought an end to his years of ease, and he had to turn back to the humpbacking that he had taught the natives.[3]

The industry he started at one time spread to Grenada, St. Lucia, Barbados, and Trinidad, but by World War II only the Bequia whal-

[3] Frederic A. Fenger, "Longshore Whaling in the Grenadines," *The Outing Magazine*, 1917, p. 678.

ers remained at the trade. The Barouallie fishermen learned to whale from the Bequia men, but they do not go after the large humpbacks (*Megaptera nodosa*), which were the staple catch of the Grenadines men but which necessitate going much farther out to sea than do the smaller blackfish.

The Barouallie whalers, however, use the same gear and techniques as those who fish for the humpback. Their boats are the same double-ended whaleboats used by the New England whaler (though, as Fenger noticed, they lost some of the gracefulness in the translation). They are twenty-two–twenty-six feet long and are manned by six crewmen—the captain and harpooner, the steersman, and four oarsmen. The boats are sprit-rigged sloops with a center- or daggerboard. Until recently, the whales were struck by hand with harpoons, but now a somewhat more modern rifle is used. About 150 fathoms of line are attached on one end to a harpoon and on the other to another iron. As the line runs out, it passes around a "loggerhead," a smooth round hardwood pin that is anchored in the afterdeck.

The whalers are, as might be expected, a "hardy crew," men who are strong and proud of their strength and endurance. They are, of necessity, usually young, mostly under thirty-five. Their trade demands great strength and flexibility, and they are conscious of this and are proud of their abilities. But they often regard themselves as caught between two forces that are beyond their control—the whale and the other people involved in the whaling operation. Thus, they talk and sing a great deal about the perfidious ways of whales and of people like the owner, the lazy man who will not get up in the morning and go whaling in the slack season, and the other whalemen who will not adhere to the necessities of cooperation in this perilous business. In short, they are conscious of the hardships of their life; they revel in their hard lot, and they talk about it, sometimes to the point of complaint.

The men are up at five or six in the morning, and they are at sea between eight and nine, where they remain until four or six. The time is much longer when a large fish is taken, for it must be brought back to shore; in such a case it may be late at night before they get home.

The usual operation is one of rowing or sailing out to the fishing ground and waiting until a sighting is made. Then there will be a good deal of excitement and commotion, especially if a school of whales is sighted. All the crewmen then devote themselves to getting over to the school as soon as possible. If it is calm, they all get to their oars and start pulling fiercely, often to the rhythm of one of their quick-tempoed shanties. It may take three-quarters of an hour or more before they get a whale in range.

When they do get close enough, they use the harpoon gun—actually a shotgun assembly affixed to a piece of inch-and-a-half steel pipe, two feet in length. Into this steel pipe is put the tightly fitting wooden stock of a harpoon, the fit being guaranteed by the addition of a couple of rubber washers. The shot is taken from the shell or cartridge, and cardboard is added in. This propels the harpoon up to fifty or sixty yards with reasonable accuracy. The maximum range is seventy to seventy-five yards. The harpooner aims in a kind of arc, estimating the progress of the whale (the harpooner is of course experienced with his gun and has learned to estimate effectively the capacity of his weapon). He is frequently accurate.

When the whale is caught it takes a great time to actually kill it and longer to cut it up and get it back to shore. Once the harpoon holds fast, the blackfish will tow the boat for as long as three-quarters of an hour to an hour, especially if it is a cock (which is what they call the male of the species). When he gets close to the boat, they throw an iron at him, a wooden-handled piece of steel, about two feet long, the steel being flattened into a sharp edge on two sides, much like a long, sharp spade. That is hurled at the whale, with the result that a great deal of blood is usually thrown about as the whale threshes. When the men finally achieve the kill, the blackfish leaps out of the water in a final move, and there is great cheering from the crew. Then the beast is cut up and brought to shore where the meat is corned and the oil is rendered in huge vats (which used to be used for sugar melting) in sheds on the beach.

Of the catch, the owner of the boat gets half. The crew divides the other half six ways—each man gets one share except the steersman, who gets two. The captain gets ten percent of the owner's share, plus his share as a member of the crew. The total income from a blackfish is commonly $120–150 West Indian currency (or $60–75 U.S.). In the past few years, the whalers usually caught around three hundred blackfish a year and about a dozen sperm whales. Meat sells at about ten to fifteen cents a pound for the blackfish, only occasionally twenty. It then retails by the vendors in town for forty to fifty cents after it has been corned or dried by the women. The price of sperm whale meat is somewhat less, since there is so much more of it. A blackfish will weigh from one-half to three tons, of which approximately half is edible meat. There is also a good quantity of oil for which there is a very fluctuating market (at present most of the best oil is bought by a small watch-manufacturing company).[4]

The sharing system creates certain antagonisms and jealousies. For instance, the men feel ambivalent toward the owners because the latter do not share the dangers of the sea. Nevertheless, they are commonly respected people in the community, and they often go out of their way to give a good deal of congratulations on a catch. Furthermore, the owner, by custom, provides free grog on such occasions.

But the owners have a responsibility to the men that they do not always live up to—to provide good equipment. When they fail to have proper line or sail or something of that sort, and especially when this prevents the men from making a catch they think they should have made, the men will do something about it. They may direct a

---

[4] In an unpublished pamphlet by H. H. Brown deposited in the Kingstown Library, the following figures are given for 1945: "Each blackfish may produce anything from 7 to 20 gallons of oil which is valued locally at $2.00 per gallon, some of which is exported; largely it is understood for medicinal purposes." In 1944, 596 gallons of "fish oil" valued at $1,139.20 were shipped to Trinidad, Barbados, and Grenada.

shanty at him, for instance, "If the line it is lame then the owner's to blame," or they may deliberately sabotage the equipment in question. For instance, if the sail is regarded as too old, the captain may let it blow up into the breeze, allowing it to luff so violently that it will shred to pieces. Then the owner is liable to become very "vex" about the whole thing and go about cursing the "niggers" who have pulled this trick on him.

There are similar reactions by the crew to the vendors, who they feel do not pay enough for the meat. Consequently, there may be occasional scenes on the beach by the whaling men to dramatize this point, which is as much to underline how dangerous their trade is as to register a complaint. The antagonism between the seamen and the vendors is somewhat modified by the fact that they are often in the same family, and thus their need to *get through* (make a living) is a shared concern. Ultimately, the major problems arise when the values of capitalism come into conflict with the values of familistic cooperation, on which the sea part of the trade is built. Judging by the talk and the songs of the men, it is the human, and especially the social, lapses which are regarded as the greatest dangers.

All these remarks are made as introduction to the talk and songs of the men themselves, so that they may be better understood. As will be seen, the whalers themselves are articulate about the problems of their employment and way of life, singing and talking about them with great perception. In the shanties sung as part of their operation, the topics of greatest importance—the whales and the non-whaling people—emerge again and again. I will, in most cases, allow the men to have their own say on these subjects. Most of the comments here, which will be given in italics, come from one captain, Alfred Mason, or from members of his crew on the days in June 1966 when I first recorded in Barouallie.[5] The songs fall roughly into three

[5] The crew consisted of: Captain Alfred Mason (age 34); Steersman—Milton Patrick (25); George Spencer (22); George John (21); Granville Richardson (23); and Conrad Harry (21).

groups: songs associated with specific whaling activities, those which talk about different types of people associated with whaling, and finally those which tell stories about some local personage.

A number of the songs directly portray the perils of whaling or some specific aspect of the whaling techniques. Typical of these is the shanty "Blow My Bully Boy, Blow My Blow," which is used after squally weather.

When the weather is squally and we taken fish, we have one that we are sing, "All through the rain and squally weather." We call the blackfish "Guinea Nigger" to feed black nigger, and we does sing about that.

"All through the Rain and Squally Weather"

Oh, squall in the morning, squall in the evening,
Hay, ay, ay.
Oh, squall in the morning, squall in the evening,
Blow my bully boy, blow my blow.

Blow Bull Johnson, blow your fibre,
Hay, ay, ay.
Oh, blow your fibre from Antigua,
Blow my bully boy, blow my blow.

Yes, she came in rimmin' the water,
Hay, ay, ay.
Oh, sandfly leg and mosquito liver,[6]
Blow my bully boy, blow my blow.

Oh, big Florita run down the river,
Hay, ay, ay.
Oh, she went down the river to hunt Guinea Nigger,
Blow my bully boy, blow my blow.

Oh, he want Guinea Nigger to feed black nigger,
Hay, ay, ay.
Oh, blow your fibre from Antigua,
Blow my bully boy, blow my blow.

Squall in the morning, squall in the evening,
Hay, ay, ay.
Oh, blow your fibre, let me hear you,
Blow my bully boy, blow my blow.

Oh, Bull Johnson, blow your fibre,

[6] Cf. "Blow Boy Blow," pp. 55–57.

Hay, ay, ay.
Oh, blow your fibre from Antigua,
Blow my bully boy, blow my blow.

Here she come with a cargo color,
Hay, ay, ay.
Oh, squall in the morning, squall in the evening,
Blow my bully boy, blow my blow.

*Another song we does sing for the same squally weather is "Oh,
My Rolling River."*

"Oh, My Rolling River"

All through the rain and squally weather,
Oh, my rolling river.

All through the rain and squally weather,
We are bound away from this world of misery.

Misery, I come to tell you,
Oh, my rolling river.
All through this rain and wind all squally,
We are bound away from this world of misery.

Salambó, I love your daughter,
Oh, my rolling river.
Salambó, this white mulatta,
We are bound away from this world of misery.

Seven long years we toiled the ocean,
Oh, my rolling river.
Seven long years, I never wrote her,
We are bound away from this world of misery.

All through the rain and squally weather,
Oh, my rolling river.
All through this rain and windy squally,
We are bound away from this world of misery.

"Misery," my captain cry out,
Oh, my rolling river.
"Solid fas'," my bowman cry out,
We are bound away from this world of misery.

I courted Sally, no pen no paper,
Oh, my rolling river.
I courted Sally with foolscap paper,
We are bound away from this world of misery.

*But mostly we does sing it after a long rowin' or coming home late
at night and we must pull hard. Then we does sing it with different
words.*

Solid fas' I come to tell you,
Hurrah, my rolling river.
"Solid fas'," our captain cry out,
We are bound away from this world of misery.

Nobody knows about our toilin',
Hurrah, my rolling river.
Only God Almighty knows about our danger,
We are bound away from this world of misery.

"Whale ahead," my little gunman cry out,
Hurrah, my rolling river.
"Solid fas'," my little captain answer,
We are bound away from this world of misery.

And on our way, she roll and shiver,
Hurrah, my rolling river.
Down in our way she sport dirty water,
We are bound away from this world of misery.

"Make her so bold," my strokeman cry out,
Hurrah, my rolling river.
"Haul an' gi' me," my centerman cry out,
We are bound away from this world of misery.

Nobody knows about our hardship,
Hurrah, my rolling river.
Our shipowner she don't knows our hardship,
We are bound away from this world of misery.

"Solid fas'," my gunman cry out,
Hurrah, my rolling river.
"Solid fas'," my little second bow'e cry out,
We are bound away from this world of misery.

Misery into the ocean,
Hurrah, my rolling river.
Misery in the deep wide ocean,
We are bound away from this world of misery.

You see, when you strike the fish, anyhow, the captain say "Solid fas'." Sometime the bowman in action already pullin' up the fish. He turn to the captain so the captain have better position to see, so sometime he say it first, but is usually the captain. Soon as somebody see the fish, 'e say "Spout-o!" And then we blackfish boys, we start to

pull, and I say "Draw-way, boys, draw way." Then the boys start to
chant dey, pulling hard. We does have special songs for that.

Emmalina girl,
Ay-ah
Come go home with me,
Ay-ah.

Relief coming,
Ay-ah
Turn a-rolling,
Ay-ah.

When we reach fifty or sixty yards, we stop becau' we does need
silence. We stop singing; when he hears some noise he would sound
and go to bottom.

White bird get up,
Ay-ah
And she break she tail,
Ay-ah.

Black bird get up,
Ay-ah
And she do de same,
Ay-ah.

Oh, me Donna,
Ay-ah
Emmalina girl,
Ay-ah.

Oh, me Donna,
Ay-ah
Girl come go with me,
Ay-ah.

White bird get up,
Ay-ah

"Blackbird Get Up"

And she shake she tail,
Ay-ah.

Black bird get up,
Ay-ah
And she do the same,
Ay-ah.

Oh, me Donna,
Ay-ah
Emmalina girl,
Ay-ah.

Oh, me Donna,
Ay-ah
Girl come go with me,
Ay-ah.

*When we meet with fish, now (the boys dem does sing it in a kin'
a 'rageous way now), "We catch 'im at las' and we tear his black ass'."
That's when we strike and kill 'im. We do a good fishing and, well,
we have a shanty we start to sing.*

"Bully, Long Time Ago"

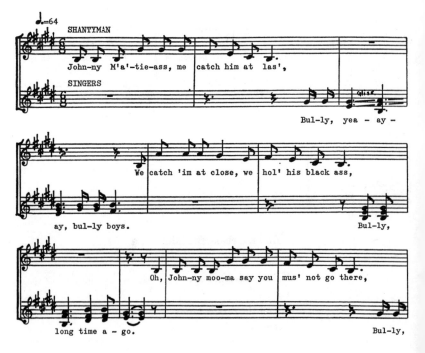

Johnny M'a'tie-ass, me catch him at las',
Bully, yea-ay-ay, bully boys.
We catch 'im at close, we hol' his black ass,
Bully, long time ago.

Oh, Johnny' mooma [mother] say you mus' not go there,
Bully, yea-ay-ay, bully boys.
Long time, a-moving time,
Bully, long time ago

Oh, long time, a hell of time,
Bully, yea-ay-ay, bully boys.
Long time, I hol' 'im at las',
Bully, long time ago.

Oh, Johnny M'a'tie-ass, I catch 'im at las',
Bully, yea-ay-ay, bully boys.
I catch 'im at close, I hol' his black ass,
Bully, long time ago.

Oh, Johnny' mooma say you mus' not blow deep,
Bully, yea-ay-ay, bully boys.
Long time, a-moving time,
Bully, long time ago.

Oh, long time, a hell of a time,
Bully, yea-ay-ay, bully boys.
Long time I hol' 'im at las',
Bully, long time ago.

Oh, Johnny' mooma say you mus' not blow deep,
Bully, yea-ay-ay, bully boys.

Long time I hol' 'is black ass,
Bully, long time ago.

Here's another shanty, like when we go to sea an' we meet the tame fishes them. You know sometime we does go off an' meet jus' wid them, can't even 'rangin' them to shoot—but anudder time you're gonna meet some and can touch them before we strike them. Well, we have a shanty we does sing about that. "Those Girls from Bermuda, They Love Us So Well."

"Those Girls from Bermuda"

Those girls from Bermuda come pay us a view
Row, row, row, my boy
An' de now as we row an' we now comin' home
Goodbye fare-you-well, goodbye fare-you-well.

Fare-you-well is the fisherman groun'
Row, row, row, my boy
If those girls from Bermuda de pay us a view
Goodbye fare-you-well, goodbye fare-you-well.

Fare-you-well, let us heave and go home
Row, row, row, my boy
Oh de now as we roam and we now coming home
Goodbye fare-you-well, goodbye fare-you-well.

Fare-you-well is the fisherman groun'
Row, row, row, my boy
And then so as we row, now we come back home
Goodbye fare-you-well, goodbye fare-you-well.

Fare-you-well Juliana, you know
Row, row, row, my boy
Well them girls from Bermuda, they pay us adieu
Goodbye fare-you-well, goodbye fare-you-well.

Fare-you-well, let us heave and go home
Row, row, row, my boy
On west'ard we row and we now coming home
Goodbye fare-you-well, goodbye fare-you-well.

De sperm whale many times attack de boat. Plenty times knock it over, punch de bottom, and sometime de men jus' swim dem becau' de boat sunk. Stove it out. Are running so dangerous. In our waters, no never get kill! But they put us down already. You see we are so skillful about it that anytime we does see a sperm whale before it get close, we prepare' already for she. So when we strike dey, if she going too fas', we cut de rope out.

One time las' week when that so, and they came right up to the boat it was so tame. Come right up an' butt on the boat dey. Sperm whale. I couldn't shoot it at all. I jus' had a goin' over it like that, but I couldn't pull the gun. If I did pull de gun it would jus' run on de boat an' smash it. An' it was I alone on the rail. I didn't take no chances at all. When we stick dem an' dey runnin' dangerous we put the line aroun' the loggerhead to check them up. The Bequia whaler call it de "Sampson Post" but we call it de "loggerhead." 'Cause de strong hol'. Sometimes when the sperm whale runnin' with speed dat t'ing trailin' fire, jus' like a cigarette lighter, sparking. This rope it will bin' them for the purpose. Jus' to wet de rope all de time, keep on wettin'.

Sometimes we does catch a sperm whale, well, we have a shanty on that. Anywhere we meet the fishes dem, we call it "Royo Groun'." We take a fish, we say it's from Royo Groun', it's a lucky ground. This Royo is a river in America, you know, Royo Grandé. It's jus' a lucky ground.

> Royo Groun' where we kill that sperm whale,
> Heave away,[7] Royo.
> Oh, Royo Groun', captain, where we boun' from,
> We are boun' from Royo Groun'.
>
> An' we are comin' home from Royo,
> Heave away, Royo.
> Oh, fare-you-well, Juliana, my boy,
> We are boun' from Royo Groun'.
>
> Royo Groun', our lucky groun',
> Heave away, Royo.
> Oh, Royo Groun' where we bid dem good bye,
> We are boun' from Royo Groun'.
>
> Royo Groun' where we kill an' come home,
> Heave away, Royo.
> Oh, captain, gunman, where we boun' from?
> We are boun' from Royo Groun'.
>
> Captain, harpooner, where we boun' from?
> Heave away, Royo.
> Oh, Royo Groun', Mason killed that sperm whale,
> We are boun' from Royo Groun'.
>
> And away, Royo,

[7] Sometimes "Heave oars."

"Royo Groun'"

Heave away, Royo.
Oh, fare-you-well Juliana my boy,
We are boun' from Royo Groun'.

Royo Groun' where we kill an' cut in,
Heave away, Royo.
Oh, Royo Groun' where we kill an' cut in,
We are boun' from Royo Groun'.

*Now when we catch the whale now, an' we pull 'im on de shore,
that's the shanty to haul 'im up. The sperm whale. We usually kill
the sperm whale or the whale-killer, the black an' white one. Those
is one the shanty to bring 'em up. One special shanty, "Yard Away,
Yard Away."*

"Yard Away, Yard Away"

Yard-o, yard-o
Bell a ring a yard-o
Yay-ay, bell a ring a yard-o.

Master dead na lef' no money
Mistress have fo' look fo' money
Yay-ay-ay, devil in a yard-o.

Yard-o, yard-o
Devil in de yard-o
Yay-ay-ay, devil in de yard-o.

Master dead na lef' no money
Mistress have to work fo' money
Yay-ay-ay, devil in de yard-o.

Yard-o, yard-o
Man came in de yard-o
Yay-ay-ay, devil in de yard-o.

Master dead na' left no money
Mistress have fo' look fo' money
Yay-ay-ay, devil in de yard-o.

Yard-o, yard-o
Devil in de yard-o
Yay-ay-ay, devil in de yard-o.

Master dead na' left no money
Mistress have fo' look fo' money
Yay-ay-ay, devil in de yard-o.

So's when they sing that shanty out, like that, haulin' and tell 'em she come.

Well is dose ol' time Africans, you know, in the same speech like how we sing it, "Bell a ring a yard-o." Well perhaps this master had like a overseer, you know, some manager because they usually have bell in every estate, you know. So this rich man dead, they say he di'n' leave no money. Well the missus have to go an' look for money.

An' a man, some man came in the yard to interrupt the mistress, you
know—I don't know what the real name they call 'im—'e have like
an attendant in the yard, you know, until this man come out the
yard-o.

Another we does sing when we have de whale on de sea, in de
water, want 'e bring it up on land, everybody haul on de rope and
sing that shanty.

"Dan-Dan-oh"

Whe'fore, wet me, Dan-Dan-oh
Dan-Dan, whip me, Dan-Dan.

Oh, dem girl, der take me shillings all
Dan-Dan-oh, whip me, Dan-Dan.

Whe'fore, wet me, Dan-Dan
Dan-Dan-oh, whip me, Dan-Dan.

Dan-Dan-oh, whip me, Dan-Dan
Dan-Dan-oh, whip me, Dan-Dan.

Whip, whip me moon a show
Dan-Dan-oh, whip me, Dan-Dan.

All dem girl they take me money gone
Dan-Dan-oh, whip me, Dan-Dan.

Whip, whip, whip me, Dan-Dan-oh
Dan-Dan-oh, whip me, Dan-Dan.

All dem girl dey take all me shillings gone
Dan-Dan-oh, whip me, Dan-Dan.

Whip, whip, whip me, Dan-Dan
Dan-Dan-oh, whip me, Dan-Dan.

All dem girl come an' take me silver coin
Dan-Dan-oh, whip me, Dan-Dan.

Whip, whip, whip me, Dan-Dan
Dan-Dan-oh, whip me, Dan-Dan.

All dem girl come an' take me money gone
Dan-Dan-oh, whip me, Dan-Dan.

Whip, whip, you whip me, Dan-Dan
Dan-Dan-oh, whip me, Dan-Dan.

Whip, oh whip, oh whip me, Dan-Dan-oh
Dan-Dan-oh, whip me, Dan-Dan.
High Whale!

When we say "High whale" we reach up, close on de san'.

After a hard haul bringing a whale in, the whole town is up and helping. The owner of the boat brings some grog, and there is much drinking and rejoicing. Sometimes when the moon is bright the cheerfulness will lead to playing singing games.

After we done finish haul up de whale, we get on the sand, we make ring-play there, you know. Just like we rejoicing then. We play all the time until we get tired and we go home and sleep. Sometimes all like two in the night we still playing. When the moon is bright den. When it is dark we done with that.

The games they play are the same ones that used to be popular throughout the island before electricity came in, as well as politics, radio, and other things that have driven neighbors and family apart. These are the ring-plays, like "There's a Black Girl in the Ring," that call for the making of a ring and the individual isolating of a performer or a couple in the middle of the ring where they do their "motions." The most popular of these seem to be "Tinnego" and "Jane and Louisa."

"Tinnego"

Deacon, Duncan, Tinnego
Tee-ay-ay, Tinnego.

When we go reach a Walabo[8]
Tee-ay-ay, Tinnego.

Deacon, Duncan, Tinnego
Tee-ay-ay, Tinnego.

Hol' on le' we go a quite Walabo
Tee-ay-ay, Tinnego.

Deacon, Duncan, Tinnego
Tee-ay-ay, Tinnego.

Deacon, Duncan, Tinnego
Tee-ay-ay, Tinnego.

Time fo' we go a Walabo
Tee-ay-ay, Tinnego.

Deacon, Duncan, Tinnego
Tee-ay-ay, Tinnego.

A we méma live at Walabo
Tee-ay-ay, Tinnego.

Deacon, Duncan, Tinnego
Tee-ay-ay, Tinnego.

Make a come a le' we go a Walabo
Tee-ay-ay, Tinnego.

Deacon, Duncan, Tinnego
Tee-ay-ay, Tinnego.

Is time fo' we go a Walabo
Tee-ay-ay, Tinnego.

*(A couple comes slowly into the ring and does the described ac-
tions, one then picking a new mate and so on.)*

[8] Wallilabou, the next town down the Leeward coast.

"Jane and Louisa"

Jane and Louisa will soon come home, darling,
Soon come home, darling, soon come home.
Jane and Louisa will soon come home,
Out of the beautiful garden.

Then I will like you to pick a rose, darling,
Take a rose, darling, take a rose.
Then I will like you to pick a rose,
Out of the beautiful garden.

Then I will like you to waltz [or walk] with me, darling,
Waltz with me, darling, waltz with me.
Then I will like you to waltz with me,
Into the beautiful garden.

These are not the only amusements the whalers have. Their days on the sea are filled with long periods in which they have nothing to do, and so they improvise their own entertainments by joking, arguing, riddling, and telling stories.

When we are out and there are no whales we make lots of jokes wid each udder. We say "Boy's nothing today. We haven't seen any-t'ing. Dey gone an' sleep. Dose girls gone asleep boys. Nothing today." We always hope dat tomorrow we meet dem early. And there we speak riddle wid one another, or tell another boy their girlfriend . . .

and all those things, making jokes on one another. We speak de rid-
dles and de Nansi stories. Just to keep them going, you know. We tell
'em about a man name Mr. Anansi.

There are a number of comic routines that are replayed under such
circumstances but that almost defy being written down because
their humor depends on actions or on paralinguistic phenomena—
strange pitch, unusual stress patterns, and so on. The following,
given by way of example, is a dialogue between a "stupidity" boy
and a man at the bus station in the market, in which the boy keeps
saying the same things over and over again, in a whining, tongue-tied
fashion. It is probably a reporting of an actual event, for any kind
of abnormality of this sort is regarded as terribly funny. If someone
has a speech defect or some physical deformity, he learns early in
life not to go out of his yard or he will be called on to entertain and
be laughed at.

> *Boy, come here.*
> *A me mooma.*
> *Boy, wha' doing in town?*
> *Mooma.*
> *Boy, whe' your shoe?*
> *A me mooma.*
> *Boy, bus go leave you now.*
> *A who dat? A poopa.*
> *Boy, a whe' your shoe?*
> *A me mooma.*
> *Boy, you really wil'.* [wild]
> *A who dat? A mooma.*
> *But whe' boy you' clothes?*
> *A who dat? A me mooma.*
> *Boy, well you all go home.*
> *A who dat? A me mooma.*
> *Boy whe' you' shoe?*
> *A me mooma.*

Boy, where you will go?
A who dat? A poopa.
That is a boy from some time ago in the country.

One of the most common amusements is the telling of "Anansi stories"—that is, any tale that might be told at a wake. The stories get their name from the spider-trickster Compé Anansi, but not all stories are told about this figure. While on the sea, the stories are naturally extended to fill up time, but the following was reported by the whalers on land and is not as elaborate a rendering because of the changed situation.

This Anansi had five children. He was so poor, but when he come home this night he had nothing to give the children them. But he had one coconut tree, so he go on this coconut tree and he begin pick some nuts. While during picking the nuts them, the nuts they fall in the sea. Well as they fall in the sea, he concentrate. Well he can't get his nuts.

Well he had a little boat and he push off the boat and go to sea looking for the nuts. And soon he dives down going to de back on the sea he met a man. That name was Mr. T'underman, soon as he go down T'underman say, "Eh, Nancy you here?"

He say, "Yes, I was picking some coconuts and all fall overboard." Well he say, "Okay, don't bother with the coconuts them. I give you a pot." So them coming back on board then and say, "Pot do for me as you used to do for your master." Well, as soon as he reach on board he say, "Pot do for me as wha' you used to do for your master." The pot come full a nice soup. He relax himself and he eat well. Eat. Good. He so bad now. He had so many children an' ain' want the children then to get some of those delicious food. He hide away the pot. Well the boys they see he come in fat every day. The children know he care nothin' 'bout [them]. Every time the wife send him, "Wha' you upsettin' me for? Wha' you gone to fo' dem chirren dem?" The wife grievin'. He comes in too fat. Grievin'. Good!

One day now, they had a son who turn a fly. When he turn a fly an' he see what he father doing. He get on the same key where the

father put down the pot. He say, "Pot do for me as you do for master."
The pot nice soup. Father eat. Soon after the father turn away, he
come but in human beings, visible again. Take the pot home. Reach
to the mother. Mother tell do the same thing. The pot start to do
develop food. Everybody eat. Well the mother was so stupid—she was
a kind wife take the pot, go to the neighborhood so she can make
food for the neighbors so the pot disappear.

When Anansi come back home—no pot. He go back to the tree
where he pick coconuts but he willfully just stand and throw all the
coconuts into the sea. And when he go down back. Said, "Oh, Mr.
T'underman, I looking for my nut. Them a fall in the sea." That time,
he was a liar then he willfully did this thing. But T'underman he
knows what Anansi did. T'underman hand out a stick. "Have a stick."
When he get on board say, "Stick do for me as do for master." He
believe he will get something else he going get now. Soon as he ready
up, driving the boat on the water soon as the hand touch so. "Praise
God I reach a boat. Stick, do for me as you does do for master." Licks!
Licks! Firesticks! Run from blood, run from stone. Pure licks! Pure
licks! He say, "Stop stick! Stop stick! Who stick is doing so?" "Lick
stick, firewood." He fling himself clean overboard and the stick jump
in the water. And the stick go back an' meet T'underman. And from
that day he learn something good. He say he will never be a covetous
man again. He will always let them take what given to him and not do
no fas'er [i.e., be thievish].

There are certain situations at sea that the whalers comment upon
in their songs, such as the following version of "Blackbird Get Up"
(see pp. 76–78), which is sung when the men are being rained on.

> Wet, messy wet
> Ay-ah
>
> Wet, messy wet
> Ay-ah
>
> Water feel a stick
> Ay-ah

When the rain come down
Ay-ah

Wet, messy wet
Ay-ah

Water feel a stick
Ay-ah

When the rain come down
Ay-ah

Water feel a stick
Ay-ah

When the rain come down
Ay-ah

Oh, crazy wet
Ay-ah

Water feel a stick
Ay-ah

When the rain come down
Ay-ah

Wringing wet
Ay-ah

Water feel a stick
Ay-ah

When the rain come down
Ay-ah.

This song can also be used to pull the boat out of the water during the rain. Actually there are a number of such songs with short choruses that can be used either for quick rowing or for pulling the boats up, like the following:

Hey, Bully Monday,
Hey boy.

"Hey, Bully Monday"

Ya' gone walk down Sal' pond,
Hey boy.

Hey, Bully Monday,
Hey boy.

Walk down Sal' pond,
Hey boy.

Hey, Bully Monday,
Hey boy.

Gone walk down,
Hey boy.

Hey, Bully Monday,
Hey boy.

Gonna walk down Sal' pond,
Hey boy.

Oh, Bully Monday,
Hey boy.

He go walk Sal' pond,
Hey boy.

Oh, Bully Monday,
Hey boy.

We go out on Sal' pond,
Hey boy.

Oh, Bully Monday,
Hey boy.

We go out down Sal' pond,
Hey boy.
    Hold 'train!

De sal' pon' is where they obtain sal' to corn de whale. Down de cays they have, down near Mayaro [one of the smaller Grenadines]. You have to work hard in sal' pon' becau' you bring a large whale you have to bring plenty salt to salt the whale. Have to work 'pon de sal' pon'.

"Little Boy Lonzo"

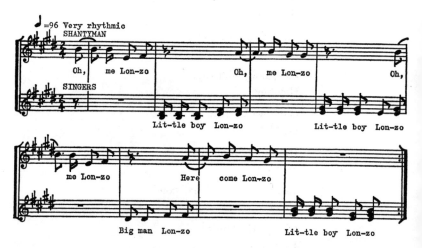

Oh, me Lonzo
Little boy Lonzo

Oh, me Lonzo
Little boy Lonzo

Oh, me Lonzo
Big man Lonzo

Here come Lonzo
Little boy Lonzo

Little boy Lonzo
Little boy Lonzo

Oh, me Lonzo
Little boy Lonzo

Lay down boy Lonzo
Lonzo, Lonzo

Lay down boy Lonzo
Lonzo, Lonzo

Little boy Lonzo
Lonzo, Lonzo

Little boy Lonzo
Lonzo, Lonzo

Little bitty Lonzo
Lonzo, Lonzo

Big man Lonzo
Lonzo, Lonzo

Big man Lonzo
Lonzo, Lonzo

Big man Lonzo
Lonzo, Lonzo

Little bitty Lonzo
Lonzo, Lonzo

Little bitty Lonzo
Lonzo, Lonzo

Etc.

The shanties given up to this point reflect the tensions that arise
in the confrontation between man and whale, as well as the tremen-
dous respect given both to the whale and to other whalers who do

their job well. But there are other problems of the trade that are commented upon in the songs. For instance, one of the recurrent situations is the inability of an owner to get a full crew for his boat. The crew, in such a situation, feels understaffed and lets the owner know this by mocking him as a "poor old man."

Sometimes if there is a owner and one going to leave the boat and he can't get nobody to go in his boat, we sing that song to him. Because he's a poor fellow he can't get nobody to go on his boat. So we usually sing this tune, just making mock on him, giving him a little fátigue.

> The poor ol' man he sick in bed,
> 'E want somebody to 'n'int [anoint] his head.
> Johnny come down with a hilo,
> The poor old man.
>
> Oh, this poor old man who couldn't say his prayers,
> 'E hold him by his lef' leg and he tap him downstairs.
> Johnny come down with a hilo,
> The poor old man.
>
> Oh, the poor old man he sick in bed,
> 'E want somebody to rub his head.
> Johnny come down with a hilo,
> The poor old man.
>
> Oh, we say so and we know so well,
> The poor old man 'e need some help.
> Johnny come down with a hilo,
> The poor old man.
>
> Oh, this poor old man he sick in bed,
> 'E want somebody to 'n'int his head.
> Johnny come down with a hilo,
> The poor old man.
>
> Oh, this poor old man who couldn't say his prayers,
> 'E hold him by his lef' leg and he tap him downstairs.

> Johnny come down with a hilo,
> The poor old man.
>
> Oh, the poor old man he sick in bed,
> 'E want somebody to take his head.
> Johnny come down with a hilo,
> The poor old man.

We does hear old old whaler singing that tune an' we never could tell what it [hilo] names.

The antagonism between whalers and owners gets even more pronounced if the equipment which the owner provides proves defective. Most commonly defective is the whaling line, which breaks after striking a whale. So the men have a special song, sung from the boats to the people on shore, which tells the story.

Now this one, when the rope is weak an' de fish bus' away from we, then we come an' sing this cau' it was the owner fault. He should have strong rope. The shanty is "Blow de Man Down."

> If the owner is lame that's the man we must blame
> Bully, ay ay blow de man down.
> If the owner is lame that's the man we must blame
> Oh, give us some time to blow de man down.
>
> If you give me some time I will treat you refine'
> Bully, ay ay blow de man down.
> If you give me some time I will treat you refine'
> Oh, give us some time to blow de man down.
>
> If you give she some rope, we will tie them like goats
> Bully, ay ay blow de man down.
> Blow the man right down to the groun'
> Oh, give us some time to blow de man down.
>
> Well, she walk with she bottle an' she wi' she glass
> Bully, ay ay blow de man down.
> Well, she walk with she bottle an' she wi' she glass
> Oh, give us some time to blow de man down.

Well, she walk with her bottle and walk with her glass
Bully, ay ay blow de man down.
And she walk with her bottle and walk with her glass
Oh, give us some time to blow de man down.

If she give her some rope we gon tie them like goats
Bully, ay ay blow de man down.
Blow the man right down to the groun'
Oh, give us some time to blow de man down.

Well, him walk with him dagger and walk with his squad
Bully, ay ay blow de man down.
Blow the man right down to the groun'
Oh, give us some time to blow de man down.

If the owner is lame that's the man we must blame
Bully, ay ay blow de man down.
If the owner is lame that's the man we must blame[9]

Oh, give us some time to blow de man down.

Even worse than the malfeasance of the owner in not providing equipment is that shown by the other boat who sees that a whale has been caught that is too large for a single boat to pull in but because of envy will not help with the job. Such an operation usually calls for cooperation, and when it doesn't come the situation calls for comment.

This one we going to sing, sometimes when we go to sea we makin' a little distress—sometimes you have so many fish it will take us too long to come ashore wi', an' all de other boys they does just leave us and come ashore an' lef' us, leave us there. An' sometimes our friends and they jus' leave us an' come ashore. Some of them does be jealous of you, they ain' so catch any, you know? So we make a shanty of that.

[9] The same song, without the owner's-blame stanzas, may be sung to announce a catch; that is the reference to the bottle and the glass, for it is expected that the owner will provide this, and there is usually something of a ceremony to the carrying of the bottle and the glass to the beach.

"Caesar, oh, Caesar"

Come see what frien' have done to frien',
Caesar, oh, Caesar.
Yes, come see what frien' have done to frien',
Oh, Thomas sailor run 'way.

Oh, 'e leave 'e wife an' 'e went to sea,
Caesar, oh, Caesar.

Oh, 'e leave 'e wife an' 'e went to sea,
Oh, Thomas sailor run 'way.

Oh, he promised to marry in the month of May,
Caesar, oh, Caesar.
Oh, he promised to marry in the month of May,
Oh, Thomas sailor run 'way.

Yes, 'e leave 'e wife and 'e went to sea,
Caesar, oh, Caesar.
Yes, 'e leave 'e wife and 'e went to sea,
Oh, Thomas sailor run 'way.

Oh, never too late and never too soon,
Caesar, oh, Caesar.
Oh, never too late and never too soon,
Oh, Thomas sailor run 'way.

Thomas leave 'e wife an' 'e went to sea,
Caesar, oh, Caesar.
Thomas leave 'e wife an' 'e went to sea,
Oh, Thomas sailor run 'way.

(Since) he promised to marry in the month of May,
Caesar, oh, Caesar.
(Yes) he promised to marry in the month of May,
Oh, Thomas sailor run 'way.

Now 'e leave 'e wife an' 'e went away,
Caesar, oh, Caesar.
Yes, 'e leave 'e wife an' 'e went away,
Oh, Thomas sailor run 'way.

Thomas whaler, . . . he leave his wife home and he went to sail.
Somewhere aroun' Bequia Coas', by the name Thomas William'. Was
in Barouallie here, really. I know him when those boys were not here.
He leave an' he go to Trinidad. His wife she die.

Another recurrent problem is getting the men to go to sea in slack
season, which also calls for sung comment and derision.

Usually our real fishing time is from January right up to August. But from August, some of the boys start to stray 'way from the boats, them. Can' hardly get sailors to go on the sea again. An' they have a song they does start to sing with that, the boys them start it, something "A Gray Goose Gone Home."

"Gray Goose Gone Home"

Solo: John dead,
All: Gray goose gone home,
      And the fox in the way of the morning.
Solo: John dead,

All: Gray goose gone home,
      And the fox in the way of the morning.

*When they gone home an' can' see them, sing that. Gray goose gone
home.*

Solo: John dead,
All: Gray goose gone home,
      And the fox in the way of the morning.
Solo: John dead,
All: Gray goose gone home,
      And the fox in the way of the morning.
      Who kill 'um, a who fo' bury 'um?
Solo: John dead,
All: Gray goose gone home,
      And the fox in the way of the morning.
      Who kill 'um, a who fo' bury 'um?
Solo: John dead,
All: Gray goose gone home,
      And the fox in the way of the morning.

*You know Mr. Fox is a cunning animal. So they claim that they are
chicken, the man say they are chicken an' Mr. Gray Goose now, he
gone home and the Fox is the way in the morning. They aren't coming down [to the boats] cau' Mr. Fox in the way. When Fox is out,
chicken no out, unh?*

*They don't come out after August becau' there don't be many fish
out on the coas' again. Goin' to another, warm water, or something.
We doesn't worry 'bout hurricanes then. We does get the forecast from
the weathercast, so we does stay 'shore.*

Another situation commented upon in a song, this time another
version of "Blow the Man Down," concerns the man who won't go to
sea and yet who comes down with his pan for some meat when the
whalers have a good catch. They refuse him by singing the song.

The fellow on shore, he don't like to go on sea. But any time come

in with the fish, he want something from me. So we make a shanty, say
"The man come seerees [serious] we won't give him a piece."

> If the owner is lame 'e de one I will blame
> Hooli-ay, blow de man down.
> If the owner is lame 'e de one I will blame
> Oh, give us some time to blow de man down.

> I catch silk on 'round head, and I wake up de dead
> Hooli-ay, blow de man down.
> Oh, de owner is lame, 'e is the guy I will blame
> Oh, give us some time to blow de man down.

> Oh that man come seerees, I wouldn't give him a piece
> Hooli-ay, blow de man down.
> Oh he stand and 'e sick with his head full of tricks
> Oh, give us some time to blow de man down.

> If he want to be partner, man, de boat not so fas'
> Hooli-ay, blow de man down.
> Oh me boat not so fas', I come through the pass[10]
> Oh, give us some time to blow de man down.

> If you give me some line, I will treat you refine'
> Hooli-ay, blow de man down.
> I will treat you refine', don't doubt me no time
> Oh, give us some time to blow de man down.

> Oh dat man come seerees, I wouldn't give him a piece
> Hooli-ay, blow de man down.
> I catch cock, cow, and calf
> But I came through the pass.

Sometimes we does have some sailors, go to sea with us, and we
want him to go today bu' he don' come at all, [and so] we go to sea
with six in the crew, but now five of us. An' when we take fish and
come back home, usually sing this shanty "Who no been out, don't

---

[10] The entrance to the harbor.

come a bay." Who hasn't been out don't come now and look for any meat.

Who no been off, no come a bay,
Bear away, Yankee, bear away.
Who no been off, no come a bay,
Oh, bear away, Yankee, bear away.
Oh, if you want, deliver your harpoon, boy,

Oh, bear away, Yankee, bear away.
Oh, Yankee doodle dandy boy,
Oh, bear away, Yankee, bear away.

Oh, if you want the gun so hardful, boy,
Bear away, Yankee, bear away.
Oh, de gun on the blank, so len' us a hand,
Bear away, Yankee, bear away.

Bear away we go,
Bear away, Yankee, bear away.
Bear away to Baltimore,
Bear away, Yankee, bear away.

Hey, away we go,
Bear away, Yankee, bear away.
Who no been off no come a bay,
Bear away, Yankee, bear away.

Oh, if you want, deliver your harpoon, boy,
Bear away, Yankee, bear away.
Oh, Yankee doodle dandy boy,
Bear away, Yankee, bear away.

Hey, stroke man and le' we go,
Bear away, Yankee, bear away.
Bear away to Baltimore,
Bear away, Yankee, bear away.

You notice in most of the shanties we have something about the American states in it? Well we learn that the Yankees was famous about whaling. Most of the songs we sing about something in America: Alabama, Baltimore, some other states somewhere.

Sometimes we go to sea and one of the harpooners struck a fish and it get away. Then the other, one of the other boats go to sea and he met on the water dead, so he bring the pieces. Then another harpooner make a shanty about it, call us the cobeau, becau' they want to kill up they chirren.

The one who gets the fish make it out on dey. Because sometimes we does be at sea and I struck a fish and get away from me. Since get away and go to bottom, we'll give it to be a los' fish. Another harpooner goes up and struck that fish, it belongs to him.

One of the frustrations of the trade is to harpoon a whale and then lose it. Should another boat then catch it, the frustration becomes much more severe, and in jest the first boat will call the second a bunch of "cobeaus," the carrion-eating black vultures of the area. They then joke that eating the meat of this rotting whale will produce a headache, even in a dog.

It does smell so bad it does give dog a headache to smell it. It was stink.

> Oh, Mr. Cobeau, you want to kill out a we [our] picking,[11]
> Oh, Mr. Cobeau want to kill out a we picking.
>
> Oh, de dog come and scent it, 'e give 'e dog a headache,
> Oh, Mr. Cobeau want to kill out a we picking.
>
> Oh, you Mister Cobeau bring back a we picking,
> Oh, Mr. Cobeau want to kill out a we picking.
>
> Oh, the shark come and eat it, 'e give the shark a headache,
> Oh, Mr. Cobeau want to kill out a we picking.
>
> Oh, Mr. Cobeau please bring back a we picking,
> Oh, Mr. Cobeau want to kill out a we picking.

Finally, many of the songs have nothing to do with whaling at all, but instead comment on local happenings and local personalities. These songs are thus in the tradition of the calypso pieces that are commonly written for Carnival performance. They almost certainly are a retention of the African traditions of praise songs and scandal songs. One of these concerns a hypocritical widow who outwardly

[11] "Picking" refers to *pickney*, or children, alluding to the cobeau's propensity to eat children; but "picking" also means "catch," in the sense of food to share out.

"Oh, Mr. Cobeau"

disdained men but who suddenly found herself pregnant (the reference is that she "missed" or "messed" on the bed).

> *This was a woman, she had one of the boats. So she used to pretend that she wasn't friendly with no persons. So somebody gave shove, you know—we call that "fee-eye," "macco" that means she done catch up with a fellow. So they make this song, see how Miss Celia*

had to be ashamed, be she lie in bed with Alibama—this man was
name Alibama.

"We Are Bound Down South Alibama"

We are bound down South Al - i - ba - ma.

Oh, Miss Celia, Miss Celia, you had 'o be ashame',
Oh, Miss Celia, oh.
Oh, Miss Celia, Miss Celia, you had 'o be ashame',
We are bound down South Alibama.

Oh, you say you no miss boy, you miss on the bed,
Oh, Miss Celia, oh.
Oh, Miss Celia, Miss Celia, you had 'o be ashame',
We are bound down South Alibama.

Oh, Miss Celia, Miss Celia, you had 'o be ashame',
Oh, Miss Celia, oh.

Oh, you say you don't miss boy, you miss on the bed,
We are bound down South Alibama.

Oh, Miss Celia, Miss Celia, you had 'o be ashame',
Oh, Miss Celia, oh.
Oh, Miss Celia, Miss Celia, you had 'o be ashame',
We are bound down South Alibama.

*There was another woman used to live over there by the bay, . . .
and de name is Miss May Mills. So they had a lot of mango. She
don't play' n' nobody, she called "Jailbait." So she used to go over
there, pick up all those mangoes, prevent any children them from
going picking them mango. And we sent in then, for she, the same
share we back. So the boys them did make a shanty, a "Flambeau"
shanty when we pulling up the whale now.*[12]

Oh, me go tell Miss Mills no fo' go back for Jailbait,
Haul away, haul away.

Oh, if a go back a Jailbait, don't take any mangoes,
Haul away, haul away.

Oh, haul away, buddy, haul away boys,
Haul away, haul away.

Oh, haul away, buddy, haul away boys,
Haul away, haul away.

Oh, woman have something a set man crazy,
Haul away, haul away.

Oh, haul away, buddy, haul away boys,
Haul away, haul away.

Oh, woman have something, 'e scent so funny,
Haul away, haul away.

Oh, 'e scent so funny and 'e sweet like honey,
Haul away, haul away.

---

[12] "Flambeau" was the nickname of the shanty-man who made up and sang
this song.

"Haul Away, Haul Away"

Oh, haul away, buddy, haul away boys,
Haul away, haul away.

Oh, tell Miss Mills no fo' go back for Jailbait
Haul away, haul away.

*'E have another shanty to dis thing, about "Monday morning when
I wake up." "Them little, little girl with big, big belly."*

"Lee-lee-o, Lee-lee"

Lee-lee, Lee-lee – o,   jus' a Be – quia.

Monday morning when I wake up
We have our whale, 'e gon 'a Bequia.
Lee-lee-o, Lee-lee
Lee-lee-o, gon 'a Bequia.
Lee-lee-o, Lee-lee
Lee-lee jus' gone 'a Bequia.

Lee-lee girl with big, big botty
And a big-big girl have little botty.
Lee-lee-o, Lee-lee
Lee-lee-o, jus' a Bequia.

Monday morning when I wake up
We have our whale, 'e gon 'a Bequia.
Lee-lee-o, Lee-lee
Lee-lee-o, gon 'a Bequia.

Little girl have big, big belly
Big-big girl have little belly.
Lee-lee-o, Lee-lee
Lee-lee girl have Bequia belly.

Not all the songs are concerned with such scandal. One concerns
a fisherman, purported to be local (but a long time ago), who sacri-
ficed part of himself so that his children would not go hungry.

*This shanty is about Sintali. He was a fisherman who was so dear
to his children that one day he went to go out fishing. He could not
get bait. But he insist that he must go to fishing and get something for
the children them. Have he cut off certain parts of his body, used them*

as bait. *We don't know it is true, but we hear so from we parents' time. Cut off 'e penis an' use 'em as bait.*

"Sintali"

Oh, Sintali, Sintali, a poor fisherman,
Sintali, I-yah [I hear], you know.
Oh, Sintali, Sintali, who went out to sea,
Oh, Sintali, I-yah, you know.

Oh, Sintali, Sintali, this poor fisherman,
Oh, Sintali, I-yah, you know.
Oh, he went out to fish but he couldn't get bait,
Oh, Sintali, I-yah, you know.

So he took off his penis and take it make bait,
Sintali, I-yah, you know.
Oh, Sintali, Sintali, the big waters man,
Sintali, I-yah, you know.

Oh, Sintali, Sintali, this fine fisherman,
Sintali, I-yah, you know.
Oh, he went out to fish and he couldn't get bait,
Sintali, I-yah, you know.

So he cut off his body and take it make bait,
Sintali, I-yah, you know.
Oh, Sintali, Sintali, a fisherman great,
Sintali, I-yah, you know.

Oh, you go out to fishing and couldn't get bait,
Sintali, I-yah, you know.
Oh, you cut off your own head and take it make bait,
Sintali, I-yah, you know.

Oh, Sintali, Sintali, a fisherman great,
Sintali, I-yah, you know.
Oh, he went out to fishing and he couldn't get bait,
Sintali, I-yah, you know.

Oh, Sintali, Sintali, what a great fishing guy,
Sintali, I-yah, you know.
Oh, 'e went out to fishing and could not get bait,
Sintali, I-yah, you know.

> Oh, 'e cut off 'e free leg and take it make bait,
> Sintali, I-yah, you know.
> Oh, Sintali, Sintali, what a great lucky boy,
> Sintali, I-yah, you know.

And, as in every West Indian tradition, there are a few songs of contempt for people in neighboring towns. The following takes aim at the girls at Rosebank, branding them as whores.

> *That shanty was made up on the people on Rosebank. He belongs to Barouallie here. He used to be down there fishing. Perhaps he ain' make it up, but he is the first person we heard sing it. Mr. Swaby Fredrick.*

> The whores on shore love sailor' man money
> Roll, roll, roll and go.
> Roll and go from Calais to Dover
> (I) spend my money on the whores on shore.

> Those Rosebank whores love sailor's money
> Roll, roll, roll and go.
> Roll and go from Calais to Dover
> (I) spend my money on the whores on shore.

Finally, it seems fitting to end this survey of West Indian shanties by giving the song sung throughout the region as an end to the proceedings—whether they be housemoving, ring-play, whaling, or *fishening.*

> *When we stay out late at night we sing a shanty late at night about "Time for Man Go Home." We be out at sea, you know, and we hear the crickets bawlin', or we be playin' ring-play dem at night, or anything, and we does sing that shanty becau' it time for man go home.*

> Oh, cricket and all a bawl, oh, Lord,
> Time for man go home.
> Oh, time for man go cover dem wife,
> Time for man go home.

Oh, time for 'gouti[13] and time for die,
Time for man go home.
Oh, cricket and all a bawl, oh, Lord,
Time for man go home.

Oh, time for man go cover dem wife,
Time for man go home.
Oh, time for 'gouti and time for dance,
Time for man go home.

Oh, cricket and all a bawl, oh, Lord,
Time for man go home.
Oh, time for man go cover dem wife,
Time for man go home.

[13] Agouti (genus *Dysprocta* or *Mypoprocta*) is a large nocturnal rodent common throughout the islands.

APPENDIX

Sources of Songs

Chapter One

p. 3. "Hanging Johnny" mentioned. This song is still sung occasionally on Nevis as "Hangman Jolly"; see "Blow My Bully Boy Blow," pp. 52–53. Hugill, 284–285; Terry I, 40–42; Frothingham, 250–251; Sharp, 56; Davis and Tozer, 54–55; C. F. Smith, 44–45; Bullen and Arnold, 23; Whall, 26; Doerflinger, 31; Colcord, 72; Harlow, *Making*, 253–254; Harlow, *Chanteying*, 47–48; King, 6; Shay, 54; Sampson, 40.

p. 4. "Johnny Come Down with a Hilo." Hugill, 266–267; Terry I, 8–9; Sharp, 19; Bullen and Arnold, 9; Colcord, 102 (from Terry); Sampson, 30; Doerflinger, 30, 72; Hatfield, 113.

p. 5. "Do My Jolly Boy." This is a version of the shanty commonly called "Johnny Boker." Hugill, 289–291; Terry I, 55; Sharp, 45; Bullen and Arnold, 30; Doerflinger, 9; Adams, 312; Colcord, 44; Frothingham, 258–259; Greenleaf and Mansfield, 339; *JFSS* V, 313; King, 13; Davis and Tozer, 64; Whall, 146; Harlow, *Chanteying*, 97–98; Trevine, 14; Sampson, 52; Shay, 28.

p. 17. "De Neger Like de Bottley oh!" Hugill, 56–57; Terry II, 66–67; Sharp, 51; Colcord, 75; C. F. Smith, 42–43; Sharp also notes a relation to "Gently Johnny my Jingalo."

Chapter Two

p. 32. "Oh, What a Hell of a Wedding." A strange rendering of a comic piece popular in the late nineteenth century, called "The Monkey Married the Baboon's Sister." The song is a parody, at least in part, of "The Frog and the Mouse." It is reported in *Folksongs*, volume 3 of *The Frank C. Brown Collection of North Carolina Folklore*, pp. 219–220. The editors provide references for a number of other American reportings.

p. 34. "Michael, Row the Boat Ashore." The version of this song which became so popular through the phonograph recording of it comes ultimately from William Francis Allen, Charles Pickard Ware, and Lucy McKim Garrison, *Slave Songs of the United States*, pp. 23–24.

p. 46. "Long Time Ago." Hugill, 97–105; L. A. Smith, 44–45; Terry II, 36–37; Sharp, 49; Doerflinger, 37–43; Colcord, 65; King, 1; Sampson, 41; Shay, 48; Frothingham, 243.

p. 47. "Fire Down Below." Hugill, 115, 519–522; Terry II, 32–33; Colcord, 117; Harlow, *Chanteying*, 123–124; Davis and Tozer, 76; Hatfield, 110.

p. 56. "Blow Boy Blow." Hugill, 224–231; L. A. Smith 38; Terry I, 32–33; Sharp, 55; Bullen and Arnold, 29; Colcord, 50–52; Harlow, *Chanteying*, 66–67; Whall, 75–76; C. F. Smith, 34–35; Davis and Tozer, 40–41; Frothingham, 244–245; Mackenzie, 264; Bradford and Fagge, 4–5.

p. 57. "Judiano." Hugill gives a related piece, 576, as does Colcord, 59.

p. 58. "Oh, Louisiana." Doerflinger, 83; Bullen and Arnold, 14; Hugill, 292, 378–379 (related); C. F. Smith, 72–73 (related).

p. 59. "Feeny Brown." More commonly "Sally Brown" or "Roll and Go." Hugill, 162, conjectures a probable West Indian origin, and gives four versions (162–165). Sharp's version combines this with "Long Time Ago." Doerflinger, 74–77; C. F. Smith, 20–21; Bullen and Arnold, 6; Colcord, 82; Whall, 65–66; Davis and Tozer, 5; Terry (pt. 1), 16–17; Sharp, 12, 33; Shay, 85–86; Harlow, *Chanteying*, 122; L. A. Smith, 48–49; Bone, 94–98; Hatfield, 111.

p. 61. "Yankee John, Stormalong." Often called "Liza Lee." Hugill, 80–81; Bullen and Arnold, 24; Sharp, 41; Colcord, 60 (from Sharp); Terry (pt. 2), 54–55.

p. 62. "Blow the Man Down." Hugill, 203–214; gives a range of variations and story types. C. F. Smith, 49–51; Bullen and Arnold, 27; Colcord, 54–59; Whall, 69–70; Davis and Tozer, 42–43; Terry (pt. 1), 34–35; Sharp, 44–45; Shay, 45; Harlow, *Chanteying*, 92–95; Doerflinger, 18–22; L. A. Smith, 18–19; 31–32; Bone, 75–82; Hatfield, 109.

Chapter Three

p. 71. "Blow my Bully Boy, Blow my Blow." See "Blow Boys Blow" in Chapter Two.

p. 73. "Oh, My Rolling River." Commonly called "Shenandoah" or "Across the Wide Missouri." Hugill, 173–176; L. A. Smith, 47–51; Bone, 104–105; Terry I, 20–21; Beckett, 6–7; Sharp, 13, 58; Whall, 1–2; Davis and Tozer, 10; Bullen and Arnold, 5, 10; Doerflinger, 78–79; Adams, 316–317; Bradford and Fagge, 16; Colcord, 82–84; Harlow, *Making*, 322–323; Harlow, *Chanteying*, 112–114; *JFSS* II, 247–248; V, 44; King, 20; Sampson, 10; Shay, 66–67; C. F. Smith, 64; Frothingham, 267–268; Mackenzie, 270.

p. 80. "Those Girls from Bermuda" ("Goodbye Fare You Well"). Hugill, 120–124; L. A. Smith, 56–57; Shay, 85; Colcord, 113–114; Bone, 117; Doerflinger, 87–88; Bullen and Arnold, 8; Davis and Tozer, 18; Harlow, *Making*, 341; Harlow, *Chanteying*, 119–122; Greenleaf and Mansfield, 336; Mackenzie, 267; Sampson, 26; Terry I, 6; Trevine, 4; Whall, 119.

p. 83. "Royo Groun'." Hugill, 88–96; L. A. Smith, 10–12, 51; Terry I, 4–5; Beckett, 2–3; Sharp, 24; Bullen and Arnold, 13; Doerflinger, 64–67; Harlow, *Making*, 321–322; Harlow, *Chanteying*, 111–112; *JFSS* V, 306; Sampson, 2; Shay, 21–23; C. F. Smith, 18–19; Trevine, 6; Whall, 51–52; Frothingham, 262–264; Mackenzie, 268–269; Hatfield, 109.

p. 103. "Gray Goose Gone Home." This comes from the animal song "The Fox and the Goose." It is found, among other places, in the *Frank C. Brown Collection of North Carolina Folklore*, vol. 3, *Folk Songs*, 178–181. The editors gave a full rundown on the printed sources.

p. 110. "We Are Bound Down South Alibama." Related to "South Australia." See Hugill, 193; L. A. Smith, 49; Doerflinger, 72; Harlow, *Making*, 219; Harlow, *Chanteying*, 33–35; Colcord, 90; Hatfield, 112.

p. 117. "Roll and Go." See notes to "Feeny Brown," Chapter Two.

p. 117. "Time for Man Go Home." May be related to "Time for Us to Leave Her." For this, see Hugill, 293–297; Terry II, 52–53; Bullen and Arnold, 8; Doerflinger, 89–90; Colcord, 119–121; Davis and Tozer, 11; Harlow, *Making*, 280, 376; Harlow, *Chanteying*, 99–100; Sampson, 29; Shay, 86–87; Trevine, 16; Whall, 50; Mansfield, 371; C. F. Smith, 74–75; Frothingham, 251–252; King, 7; *JFSS* V, 36.

BIBLIOGRAPHIC NOTES

to the Songs, Rhymes, and Story

Because a major part of the argument of this monograph turns on the relationship between the contemporary West Indian and the older Anglo-American repertoires, it seems important to indicate where these songs have previously been reported in print. No attempt at complete bibliographical notes has been made, however, as I did not have access to a number of peripheral publications. If an item is not annotated here, it means that I found no reference to the song in the literature; in some cases, this may seem strange, since a song may be very much in the "mold" of the Anglo-American tradition (as in "Bear Away, Yankee, Bear Away Boy" on p. 54). The references which I have been able to consult and to which I will refer are the following:

Abrahams, Roger D. "Public Drama in Two West Indian Islands." *Trans-Action*, June–July 1968.

Adams, Captain R. C. *On Board the Rocket*. Boston: D. Lothrop and Co., 1879.

Alexander, Captain J. E. *Transatlantic Sketches*. London, 1833.

Beckett, Mrs. Clifford. *Shanties and Forebitters*. London: J. Curwen and Sons, Ltd., 1914.

Beckford, William. *A Descriptive Account of the Island of Jamaica*. London, 1790.

"Beke, X." *West Indian Yarns*. Demarara and London, 1890.

Bone, Capt. David W. *Capstan Bars*. New York: Harcourt, Brace and Co., 1932.

Bradford, J., and A. Fagge. *Old Sea Chanties*. London: Metzler and Co., Ltd., 1904.

Bullen, Frank T., and W. F. Arnold. *Songs of Sea Labour*. London: Orpheus Music Publishing Co., 1914.

Colcord, Joanna C. *Songs of American Sailormen*. New York: W. W. Norton, 1938.

Davis, Frederick J., and Ferris Tozer. *Sailors' Songs or "Chanties."* London: Boosey and Co., Ltd., n.d.

Doerflinger, William Main. *Shantymen and Shantyboys*. New York: Macmillan, 1951.

Fenger, Frederic A. "Longshore Whaling in the Grenadines." *The Outing Magazine*, 1917.

Folk Songs. Volume 3 of *The Frank C. Brown Collection of North Carolina Folklore*. Edited by Henry M. Belden and Arthur Palmer Hudson. Durham, N.C.: Duke University Press, 1952.

Frothingham, Robert. *Songs of the Sea and Sailors' Chanteys*. Cambridge, Mass.: Houghton, Mifflin, 1924. (From King.)

Greenleaf, Elizabeth B., and Grace Y. Mansfield. *Ballads and Sea Songs of Newfoundland*. Cambridge, Mass.: Harvard University Press, 1933.

Harlow, Frederick Pease. *Chanteying Aboard American Ships*. Barre, Mass.: Barre Gazette, 1962.

——. *The Making of a Sailor*. Salem, Mass.: The Marine Research Society, 1928.

Hatfield, James Taft. "Some Nineteenth Century Shanties." *Journal of American Folklore* 59 (1946): 108–113.

Hugill, Stan. *Shanties from the Seven Seas*. London: Routledge and Kegan Paul, 1961.

JFSS–Journal of the Folk-Song Society. London, 1899–1931.

King, S. H. *King's Book of Shanties*. Boston: Oliver Ditson, 1918.

Kingsley, Charles. *At Last: A Christmas in the West Indies*. London and New York, 1872.

[Lanaghan, Mrs.] *Antigua and the Antiguans, A Full Account of the Colony and Its Inhabitants from the Time of the Caribs to the Present Day, Interspersed with Anecdotes and Legends*. 2 vols. London, 1844.

Mackenzie, R. W. *Ballads and Sea Songs from Nova Scotia*. Cambridge, Mass.: Harvard University Press, 1928.

McQuade, James. *The Cruise of the Montauk*. New York, 1855.

Murphy, Robert Cushman. *A Dead Whale or a Stove Boat*. Boston: Houghton Mifflin, 1967.

——. *A Logbook for Grace*. New York: Macmillan, 1947.

Sampson, John. *The Seven Seas Shanty Book*. London: Boosey, 1927.

Sharp, Cecil J. *English Folk-Chanteys*. London: Simpkin Marshall, Ltd., Schott and Co., Ltd., 1914.

Shay, Frank. *American Sea Songs and Chanteys*. New York: W. W. Norton, 1948.

Smith, C. Fox. *A Book of Shanties*. London: Methuen and Co., Ltd., 1927.

Smith, Laura Alexandrine. *The Music of the Waters*. London: Kegan Paul, Trench and Co., 1888.

St. Clair, Thomas Staunton. *A Residence in the West Indies and America*. London, 1834.

Terry, Richard Runciman. *The Shanty Book*. 2 parts. London: J. Curwen and Sons, 1921, 1926.

Trevine, Owen. *Deep Sea Shanties*. London: J. B. Cramer and Co., 1921.

Wentworth, Trelawny. *The West India Sketch Book*. 2 vols. London, 1834.

Whall, Capt. W. B. *Sea Songs and Shanties*. Sixth edition, enlarged. Glasgow: Brown, Son, and Ferguson, 1927.